The Collision Code

Harness Serendipity, Build Life-Changing Connections.

The Collision Code

Unlock possibilities, spark meaningful relationships & transform chance into moments that truly matter.

James Eder

Praise for James Eder's
The Collision Code

Opportunities don't just happen—you create them through the people you meet. *The Collision Code* shows why saying yes to connections can change everything.

Shaa Wasmund MBE, Entrepreneur & Best Selling Author

You can't control luck. What you can control is your odds of getting lucky. With practical wisdom and relatable stories, *The Collision Code* is an essential read for anyone looking to unlock the potential of everyday moments and manufacture serendipity.

Rory Sutherland, Vice Chairman of Ogilvy, Author of Alchemy

The Collision Code is authentic, inspiring, relatable!

Dr Samuel Mwaura, Lecturer at the University of Edinburgh

The Collision Code is an essential read for entrepreneurs, offering practical advice on building connections that can transform your business. It's a brilliant guide to unlocking opportunities and creating meaningful relationships.

Emma Jones, Founder of Enterprise Nation

The Collision Code is a must-read in our digital age—reminding us that real magic happens in face-to-face connections.

Thomas Power, Entrepreneur & Founder

Whilst many attempts have been made to use technology to enable people to connect based on location and proximity none have truly succeeded. Whilst entrepreneurs will keep innovating, *The Collision Code* reminds us that real magic happens when we put down the tech and return to genuine human connection.

Mike Butcher MBE, Editor-at-Large, TechCrunch

So much of my achievements in life have been sparked by "random" collisions. I love James Eder's concise guide to codify the process.

Zoe Cunningham, Technologist and Film Producer

Great things happen when minds collide—*The Collision Code* shows how connections spark ideas, growth, and opportunity.

Michael Acton Smith, Entrepreneur & Co-Founder of Calm

The Collision Code captures the essence of what makes AIESEC thrive—authentic connections and transformative opportunities. It's an inspiring guide for anyone looking to create meaningful relationships that drive impact and growth.

Lionel Simons, Founder of AIESEC UK

The Collision Code is an inspiring read as James demonstrates and gives some insight into how we might seize with both hands every opportunity life has to offer.

James Shaw, Former AIESECer, New Zealand Climate Change Minister

At the heart of every business lies the power of human connection, which can determine its success or failure. *The Collision Code* illuminates how to forge unexpected connections and is an inspiring read for founders aiming to create a network that fuels their growth.

Anthony Eskinazi, Founder and CEO of JustPark

In *The Collision Code*, readers gain invaluable insights into forging unexpected connections that can drive business success. A must-read for anyone aiming to expand their networks and seize new opportunities.

Justine Roberts CBE, CEO at Mumsnet

The Collision Code offers a fresh perspective on making meaningful connections, much like *Getting Things Done* simplifies productivity. It's a practical guide to navigating the moments of serendipity that shape our lives, helping you turn chance encounters into purposeful relationships. I've spent my career following this advice: the greatest things you experience will come directly (or almost) from stepping out of your comfort zone to engage with someone you've never met before. A compelling read for anyone looking to align their connections with their goals.

David Allen, Founder and Author of Getting Things Done

Entrepreneurship is all about stepping outside your comfort zone. *The Collision Code* shows that the magic happens when we connect, collaborate, and embrace unexpected opportunities—because no great idea happens in isolation.

Sahar Hashemi OBE, Entrepreneur & Author, Anyone Can Do It

The Collision Code brilliantly captures how genuine connections can transform our personal and professional lives, a truth I've experienced firsthand and one that resonates deeply with me.

Gregor Lawson, Co-Founder of Morphsuits

The most impactful ideas come from the people who challenge your thinking. *The Collision Code* is a reminder that connection fuels innovation and progress.

Sam Conniff, Entrepreneur, Founder & Author

Business, like a great journey, is all about who you meet along the way. *The Collision Code* highlights how the right connections can change your course, open new opportunities, and help navigate challenges you never expected.

Gary Beckwith, Entrepreneur & Author,
How to Make A Million in Business

In facing my own health crisis, I learned that life's most profound moments hinge on the connections we create and the choices we make. *The Collision Code* delivers a stirring message: don't wait for a wake-up call to start living with purpose. Through heartfelt stories and actionable insights, James reminds us that genuine relationships are the key to unlocking both personal fulfilment and boundless opportunities.

Sherry Coutu CBE, Serial entrepreneur, Investor & Board Director

The Collision Code is a masterclass in turning chance encounters into life-changing opportunities. Through relatable stories it captures the magic of serendipity and provides the foundations to make everyday interactions count.

Matt Kingdon, Co-Founder ?What If! Innovation, author of The Science of Serendipity: How to unlock the promise of innovation.

In *The Collision Code*, James reveals how opportunities are hidden in plain sight, waiting to be unlocked—sometimes with nothing more than a simple 'hello.' Through relatable stories and real-world examples, including moments from Student Beans' journey, he shows how meaningful connections and conversations can shape success.

Michael Eder, Co-Founder, Student Beans | CEO, Pion

There are few things more important in our lives than the personal relationships we develop & nurture. *The Collision Code* highlights the power of connections to inspire, develop, create & transform leaders in every context and provides a crucial guide to deepen and enrich our relationships at every level.

Sherilyn Shackell, Founder of The Marketing Academy

Copyright © 2025 by James Eder

All rights reserved. No part of this book may be reproduced or used in any manner without written permission of the copyright owner except for the use of quotations in a book review.

For more information, contact:
hello@thecollisioncode.com

FIRST EDITION

978-1-80541-749-1 (paperback)

978-1-80541-806-1 (hardback)

978-1-80541-748-4 (ebook)

www.thecollisioncode.com

Dedications

The Collision Code is part reminder as to how short life is. None of us know how long we have so it's important to make the most of every day.

To those who are no longer with us on this Earth:

My grandparents Arthur Levin, Alice Levin, Hans Eder and Helga Eder.

To those who I was thankful to spend time with:

Andrea Elliot	Guiseppe Yule
Andrew Darnhill	Kenneth Durham
Andrew Keane	Lorraine Peters
Benedict Romain	Michaela Wells
Betsy Joseph	Ronald Moray
Brent McDaneld	Sandy Turow
Celine Naude	Steve Legge
Lord David Young	Suzy Huggett
Derek Draper	Sydney Levinson
Dean Beeson	Talya Singer
Dionne Antrobus	Tony Roberts

"If there ever comes a day when we can't be together, keep me in your heart, I'll stay there forever."

Winnie the Pooh

Thank You for Your Donation

Thank you for buying a copy of *The Collision Code*. Your purchase is supporting two wonderful charities:

British Heart Foundation

Cardiomyopathy UK — the heart muscle charity

The Collision Code was written for a number of reasons, not least to raise awareness of a number of causes close to my heart. The British Heart Foundation, together with Cardiomyopathy UK, who have supported my heart health journey and all those living with cardiomyopathy continue to research and give us a brighter future. I know the journey so far would have been much harder had it not been for them. Ten percent of the profits of this book will be donated to these charities. I (and I am sure they and all the recipients of their help) am grateful for your support. You can find out more about the brilliant work they do here:

https://www.bhf.org.uk/
https://www.cardiomyopathy.org/

A Related *Collision Code* Story

At my friend's fortieth birthday I was speaking to a couple as I was sharing stories about my adventures and travels. They were energised by the conversation, at the same time, I often feel if I don't share my heart condition people only have half the story. So I mentioned I had Hypertrophic Cardiomyopathy and Roisin who I was talking to couldn't believe it. She asked if I had a defibrillator, which I do. She then went on to share her dad, James (Jim) McParland, was personally recruited by Dr Pantridge, the renowned cardiologist, to work as a cardiac engineer in Belfast's Royal Victoria Hospital. He was one of the team of experts who developed the portable defibrillator in the 1960s and was integral to its technical function and development. Roisin and her sisters Leontia, Jacinta and Orlagh are so proud of the legacy he has left. This is just one of many developments where I am so grateful for the research and the people who've come before me that enable me and so many others to live their best lives. This charitable donation is in memory of Jim.

Contents

Foreword 1

Preface 3

Introduction 7

Part I : Getting Going 25

Part II : Making Connections 113

Part III : Moving Forward 167

Part IV : Resources 259

Acknowledgements 295

Biography 309

Foreword

On 26 August 2003, an unexpected email landed in my inbox. It was from James*, a stranger at the time, who had just been given a copy of my book, *The Naked Leader*, at Heathrow Airport before boarding his flight. His message stood out—authentic, intriguing and brimming with opportunity. Though my initial instinct was to decline his request, something about his approach made me pause.

James, as I now realise, was unconsciously applying the principles of *The Collision Code*. He gave himself the permission to reach out, showed the confidence to connect, and provided the context that made his email impossible to ignore. What followed was a meeting that sparked over two decades of collaboration, support and shared opportunities.

This is the magic of collisions—the moments that seem ordinary but can transform into extraordinary relationships. And this book will show you exactly how to embrace and create those moments in your own life.

Before Reading *The Collision Code*...

I shared the same fears as many people—the thought of stepping into a crowded room felt daunting. I'd often stand near the door or pretend to be on my phone, hesitating to approach anyone, as if I didn't belong. Or being introduced to new people—the fear was always the same—not knowing what to say or how to start a conversation. This held me back from countless connections, interactions and opportunities.

After...

Now, I have quiet confidence, embracing each encounter with ease. James' practical steps have helped me create my own personal "collision mantra". Using open-ended questions to break the ice, focusing entirely on the other person, and truly listening have become second nature.

Thank you, James, for empowering me to engage with purpose and build meaningful relationships daily.

David Taylor, author of global best-selling Naked Leader books

* See the appendix for the email James wrote to David in 2003 and the reply.

Preface

Connecting the Dots: Why It's Time for *The Collision Code*

In October 2020, as the world battled Covid, my body sent me a warning. My Apple watch alerted me to a racing heart—170 beats per minute while I was at rest. It was clear something was very wrong. I contacted my doctors, and after a series of tests, they confirmed it: my heart rhythm had shifted, I had atrial fibrillation. For years, I had been living with the heart condition hypertrophic cardiomyopathy, but this felt like a new and urgent phase.

At age thirty-seven, my doctors were suggesting a heart transplant, but I wasn't ready. The average life expectancy post-transplant is only eleven years. Some beat the odds, but I wanted more time with my own heart. I struggled with the decision, knowing that my heart was slowly failing, yet holding on to the hope that I could manage it, that I could keep going.

In the months that followed, I had moments of doubt, fear and even joy. When I found myself able to ski again—something I thought my health might take from me—it gave me a glimmer of hope. But the reality was always there, lurking. The challenge of living with a failing heart is a constant tightrope walk, balancing between when to push forward and when to surrender to the inevitable.

As I was sitting waiting for the prognosis from the doctors, I knew I had to get this book on paper. The question I've had to wrestle with is: when is the right time to act? Not just with my health, but in life. Too often, we wait until something forces us to make a change. But what if we didn't? What if we lived with intention, choosing to collide with the things that matter now, rather than waiting until it's too late?

This book is my way of sharing that realisation. Life is fragile, unpredictable and often shorter than we expect. But we have the power to choose how we spend our time. I hope the stories inspire you to act now, to live fully, and to create and embrace the collisions that bring meaning to your life.

Once I decided this book needed to happen I shared with my network that I was looking for help and so began the conversations with friends, editors, writers and agents. After an introduction from Rachel Davies to John Monks I was then introduced to Cate Caruth who helped refine the first draft.

It was then on 29 June 2023, old friends Matthew Stafford and Katie Lewis were launching their book: *Find Your 9others*. 9others is a network where you meet nine others for dinner to share business challenges often starting with the question "What's keeping you up at night?" It was here I asked Matthew how he got the book together. He shared that he had connected with Robbie Dale who I knew from

Preface

The Marketing Academy, and we had already worked together on the FriendlyFriday campaign. Not only that, Matthew and he had originally connected on Causr, as one of the first users on the platform I had built. (You'll read more about The Marketing Academy, FriendlyFriday and Causr in the book.)

Reconnecting with Robbie was pivotal. Over the best part of 2024, he helped me refine, rewrite and shape my narrative into what you hold in your hands today. I'm deeply grateful for his talent and dedication in turning *The Collision Code* into a reality.

Thank you for reading and welcome to *The Collision Code*.

Introduction

> Why do people connect?
> What stops them connecting?
> What happens when we connect?

Hi, I'm James, and I'm what people like to call a "people person". For as long as I can remember, I've thrived on meeting others, learning their stories and discovering what makes them tick. But more than just enjoying these moments of interaction, I've been captivated by a bigger question: what *really* drives human connection?

As social beings, connection is hardwired into our very nature. Yet, in today's fast-paced, hyper-digital world, we often find ourselves more disconnected than ever. It's one of the great paradoxes of our time: while we've never been more virtually connected, many of us feel isolated, missing out on the rich, meaningful interactions that truly allow us to thrive. Loneliness, in fact, is becoming the next big epidemic—and I'm determined to change that.

Not just because I believe that connection is crucial to society's happiness and wellbeing, though that's certainly true. And not just because I've founded a successful business on this very premise, though that's also a fact. But because connection has been the key to every meaningful opportunity and relationship I've ever had.

This book, then, is about the art of making connections—both in the literal sense of meeting and engaging with others, and in a broader sense, connecting the dots in life that can lead to greater opportunities. Most importantly, it's about reconnecting with ourselves in a way that brings fulfilment and purpose.

My goal isn't just for you to *enjoy* this book, but to find real value in it. I hope that by sharing my experiences, you'll uncover your own path to new possibilities, richer relationships and a deeper sense of satisfaction in your life.

And more than that, I hope you'll be inspired to take what you learn and pass it on. When we foster genuine connections, we open the door to incredible things, not just for ourselves, but for others too. Together, we can create a ripple effect of positive change.

So, thank you for choosing to spend your time with me. Let's explore the power of connection—together.

James Eder

March 2025

Collisions?

No, this isn't a book about crashes or anything else painful. Yet collisions really are at the heart of everything I want to tell you about. Given that, I want to start by defining how I think about this word, helping you to understand *The Collision Code*.

When two things collide, they take off in different directions. Think of balls on a snooker table. There's the white ball heading along in a straight line, minding its own business until click, it hits a red ball. The red ball takes off somewhere new, and the white ball has its trajectory changed forever.

This is what I mean by collisions. Because this is what happens to all of us at one time or another, and it's something I believe we should value and even seek to create more of. We move through life doing things, meeting people and going places and along the way we bump into other people doing things in their own way. That experience teaches us things, gives us new perspectives and presents opportunities. Or sometimes not. But without those collisions we're just that white ball trundling along in one direction, potentially forever, with nothing to ever set us on a new course.

And while "collision" can have a negative connotation, I am very much one for finding what's good and valuable in something that seems otherwise pointless, or negative. In that sense, I've sought to think of my collisions as always for my benefit, even if it doesn't seem that way at the time.

As you'll discover in this book, I once thought the solution to these problems was to make better use of the technology we've come to rely on every day. But as I hope you'll see through the examples in this book, I now think this is the opposite of what we need to do. So, as you read, keep in mind this mantra: put your phone down, look up and start colliding and connecting. We already have everything we need, but we sometimes need a little reminder to get going.

In this book I want to share with you my journey from my first forays into entrepreneurship to today. And I want to show you the collisions that set me on new courses, gaining momentum and shaping me along the way.

Let's start at the beginning…

The Beginning

It all began with the long-running children's TV show *Blue Peter* and the much celebrated "bring and buy sale". I'd always been fascinated by the idea of making something from nothing, or buying, selling and making money, but I had no idea how that could happen. Now I had a blueprint.

A bring and buy sale is simple: people bring things, others buy them, all the money goes to a good cause. Across the country these events were taking place spearheaded by *Blue Peter*'s latest charitable campaign, and I wanted to be part of it.

So, aged just ten years old, and with all the confidence and energy of someone who doesn't know better, I threw myself into my first entrepreneurial endeavour.

The first step was to gather things, from home first, but then further afield. It was easy to ask school mates, but I also decided to ask around the neighbours. As items came in I had fun assessing items, pricing them up and preparing for the event itself.

While finalising everything, I knocked on a few more neighbours' doors. One turned out to be the owner of Sketchleys, at the time a national brand of dry cleaners. I had no idea, nor did my parents. It's funny who might be right under your nose. He contributed a huge box of safety pins, coat hangers, sewing kits, suit carriers and more, adding a really professional air to proceedings. The sale was a huge success.

So, as you do, I thought, *What next?*

* * *

When my older brother, Michael, chose to do GCSE photography, we set up a dark room in our house for him to develop his work. At this time, we also had a Dalmatian called Smartie. The two combined to not only teach me some valuable lessons, but to help me understand the process by which I was able to make more connections.

It struck me around this time that people generally don't talk to each other. That's the default position. It's not a groundbreaking insight, but it fascinated me. What fascinated me specifically, however, was the behaviour change when a baby or animal was brought into the equation.

While out walking Smartie, people felt there was suddenly permission to start a conversation with me. "Isn't she beautiful!", "How old?", "What's her name?".

Spotting this, and thinking about this dark room we'd just created, I struck on an idea I borrowed from theme parks. At a key point on the log flume or rollercoaster, theme parks take a photo of you as you pass. At the end of the ride, you can choose to buy that photo as a memento. So why not do the same with people's dogs?

Michael and I formed M&J Photos, made some plans and set to work. Using the local parks as our go to, I asked owners if I could take photos of their dogs and them. If they liked them, then they could buy them. If not, that was OK. I had several conversations and it seemed to go down well, so we started taking photos. It was always really satisfying returning the following week with prints in hand and finding dog owners happy to part with real money for a photo of their prized pup.

Alas, it was a short-lived venture. I didn't have the patience to cope with the ups and downs at the time, and we wrapped up after one disastrous snowy day. I had taken what I thought were some great pictures in a magical setting, but when I went to develop the film I used the wrong combination of chemicals. Everything was lost, and we somewhat lost heart after that.

These things happen, but that didn't matter. I'd started.

* * *

I'm one of five with two older brothers ahead of me at University College School, (UCS) the school we attended. I remember, quite vividly, watching both of them take part in Young Enterprise, the scheme designed to give students an opportunity to set up a business while at school, when they reached sixth form.

This was more than an extra-curricular activity to me. It was the education I craved. A structured opportunity to put my ideas into action and to have the permission to spend school time building something that could even make a bit of money.

And so, as I started A levels, I waited patiently for the assembly announcement that would launch my business career. But it didn't come. Weeks went by and, frustrated, I eventually sought out the teacher, Mr Youlden, who usually ran the programme. I was told that, due to staff shortages, it wouldn't be possible to run the Young Enterprise scheme this year.

This was the moment I discovered that I don't take no for an answer. This was unfair! It was unjust! And I was determined to do something about it.

I managed to convince the headmaster, Mr Durham, that if I could find another teacher willing to supervise the programme that it would take place. The saviour was my design and technology teacher, Mr Haggar, who I convinced to sign some paperwork and trust me to get on with it. Fortunately, as a dedicated and easy pupil, he did. Paying attention in class was paying off.

With the structure in place, I now had to recruit people onto the scheme. I was nervous standing up in front of the whole school at assembly and thought few would turn up, but to my amazement over fifty were at the first meeting. From this group we formed two teams charged with coming up with an approved business idea to bring to life (the teachers still had board level powers!).

Our team's big idea was needanumber.co.uk, a web directory for local services. It sounds so obvious writing in 2024, but in 1999 this was new and untested territory for small businesses. It was the age of dial-up internet, and a "smartphone" was just one that looked nice on a console table. We called ourselves Chrome Enterprises to represent the diversity of our ideas and to complement our main venture. We ran smaller projects selling branded umbrellas and T-shirts to parents, and croissants from Louis, the local Hungarian patisserie in the tuck shop (at a ridiculous margin). The money we earned went into our dot com dream.

One Friday I went with a friend to visit some local shops to drum up business. I'll always remember one particular store where no sooner had we opened the door than we received an immediate and stinging rebuke: "Get out! Whatever you're selling GET OUT OF MY SHOP!"

It would have been tempting, prudent even, to just leave. But I believed in our idea, and I believed it would be a genuinely useful solution for this shop owner. I pushed on, explaining that I understood her response and that I also understood her need to make money from her business. Once she saw that we had something potentially useful and were only charging a nominal fee (and that all profits would go to charity) she signed up.

This experience has stuck with me ever since, and I recall it whenever I have to do something outside of my comfort zone. Inspired by that experience in the shop, I often ask myself what's the worst and what's the best thing that might happen in a given situation. In the case of the shop it was "get shouted at" versus "get a sale". The question you have to ask yourself is whether the upside is worth the potential downside. It's natural for your mind to be drawn to the negatives and to try to avoid them, but it's important to have sight of the positives too to make proper, considered decisions. Some of my biggest successes have come from thinking this way.

One of the stores I signed up for Needanumber was Waterstones in Hampstead. We reached the inner London finals of the Young Enterprise competition and one of the judges was Dame Julia Cleverdon, who was Chief Executive of Business in the Community at the time. Julia spotted that Waterstones was one of the businesses we were working with and it turns out that it was her brother Francis who was the manager at the local branch that we had signed up to our service. Despite not winning that part of the competition I remember her saying that she was very impressed and anyone who was able to sell anything to her brother deserved to be successful.

As an afterword to this story, there were fifty of us in total that took part in the programme, and all have gone on to have their own successes. But I want to mention a couple of people in particular here who were instrumental to this project. Our web programmer and designer, Anthony Eskinazi, went on to found JustPark "the Airbnb for parking" helping people rent out a car parking space, such as a driveway, to others. It was recently acquired. The other is Musa Tariq whose incredible leadership journey in marketing has taken him from Nike to Burberry, Apple and Airbnb. I often think what perhaps would have been different had we not gone down this earlier entrepreneurial path.

Andersen Consulting provided a number of mentors to the programme who provided an external perspective helping us navigate the way to get an idea successfully off the ground. We had been matched with Neel who went on to work on Nectar, Google and is currently the chief product officer of IRIS Software Group. There was then Leanne who went on to be a coach, trainer and consultant in organisational development—I've kept in touch with both of them and Leanne has been a core part of my support network whilst running Student Beans and is still involved in supporting the leadership team nearly twenty-five years later.

I'm so grateful to my teachers, the school, Nicola Garcia who was the Young Enterprise programme co-ordinator for Inner London and everyone at Young Enterprise for making these opportunities for all of us. I'm also so grateful for Francis and all those individuals behind the businesses who agreed to a listing on the website, as well as those who didn't. Each of those conversations for the website helped build my experience and confidence one signup or rejection at a time. The practical approach of learning by doing is still, I believe, one of the most important ways young people can develop and grow. The experience really lay the foundations for what was to come. If you ever get the opportunity to participate or support Young Enterprise in any way I can't recommend it more highly.

Reflection Time: Ask yourself, what's the worst thing that can happen, and what's the best thing that might happen in a given situation.

Life Lessons

The three stories you've just read were my earliest experiences of entrepreneurship, not that I really thought of it that way at the time. Back then, as a teenager, I simply thought I was doing what we're all made to do: connecting with the world by trying things that interested me. I was—as I suppose is obvious to anyone that's spent any time with young people—simply colliding into as much as I could, and having great fun doing it.

But there was more to it. And looking back through the decades since, I can start to see that even at this earliest stage I was building a foundation for everything that would come later. Yes, I made mistakes and sought to learn from them, but more than that, I started to develop a simple and repeatable framework that I would find myself applying over and over again as the years went by. A code on how to have more collisions.

I want to lay it out up front, so you can read the rest of this book with this in mind. Indeed, even if you don't make it further into the book, I want to make it my mission to share this thinking with as many people as possible.

The Collision Code: My Philosophy

I have a simple philosophy: the Collision Code. The more we connect with each other, the more good things we can make happen, together. Or, to put it in the terms we've been using, the more we collide, the better it gets.

Introduction

This is all well and good as an idea, but what does it look like in practice?

It's easy for me to invite you to make more collisions, but I know it's often much harder for people to actually do. Which is why I want to start this book by giving you a simple framework and model, known as the Collision Code, I've used for decades to help me make relevant, appropriate and helpful collisions. It was forged in those earliest experiences I've just shared; the simple combination of things that have made it much easier for me to make connections.

Permission
Confidence
Context

Permission is underpinned by confidence, both of which form a solid foundation to take advantage of the right contexts. Let's explore what we mean by each of these elements of the Code.

Permission

People often don't think they have permission to say hello or ask a question, which, to me, is nuts. We're social creatures and by extension that permission is inherited; it doesn't need to be given. That doesn't mean you have permission to harass people, or engage with people on only your terms, of course, only that as human beings we are built to connect. It's what makes society possible. It's what makes life worthwhile. You *do* have permission, and it's the context that allows you to exercise it. If you still don't feel like you've got permission then you can use the context of reading this and me. I'm literally giving you the permission to say, "I read this book and it was all about helping people connect more easily. Do you mind if I say hello?" That might seem unnatural but as you continue to read the book I trust you'll see the simple power of saying hello and the ripple effect it can have. This brings me on to the next part of the Code.

Confidence

It's true that you need to have the confidence to approach someone, even with the right context. But that's something only you can develop. Real confidence comes from experience. Not bravado or arrogance or self-importance, but strong, subtle confidence. It's the experience of asking, "What's the worst that can happen?" It's the experience of knowing that you'll find something to say. It's the trust you know you're reading a situation properly. Which means it's not something you're born with. It's something you develop and cultivate over time simply by trying. You start small, and you build from there. But it's context that will allow you that experience.

Context

By pure definition, context refers to the circumstances, background or environment that surrounds a particular situation, event or idea, helping to give it meaning. It provides the "big picture" that makes something clearer or easier to understand.

For the purposes of this book and the Collision Code, the way I think about context is simply, "What's happening right now that allows me to make a connection without making others feel uncomfortable?" I have found this to be a repeatable process that's respectful and generates great results. So, for me, I am always in this state of mind. If I'm walking somewhere, sitting somewhere, in a group conversation, at an event or anywhere else, I'm looking for a contextual hook to make a connection.

Coming up in the book you'll read about the scenario where someone was holding a resume in their hand which led to a conversation and a job offer. People shared a taxi to the airport when a train was cancelled as they had their luggage with them. I heard a muffled announcement over the loudspeaker at a tube station which gave me the context to ask the person next to me a question who turned out to be the exact person I needed to speak to in relation to a business opportunity I had identified just earlier that day.

In the stories you've already read, the context should be clear. The bring and buy sale gave me a reason to knock on neighbours' doors and a ready-made explanation to handle any questions. Taking photographs of dogs came from the context that it's very normal, expected even, to interact with others while out walking your dog. The Young Enterprise project gave a platform not only to recruit students, but to sell to parents and local businesses.

As you read this book I want you to look at how I took the context and turned it into an opportunity to collide. Often you'll see that other people, sometimes hundreds of others, were in the same context, but didn't collide.

I believe one of big reasons for not colliding and making a connection is them simply not seeing or not looking for the context. They might want to make a connections, but too many hope that will come simply from attending a networking event or keeping going through life. Colliding more is something that requires active participation.

The rest of this book looks at ways I've turned context to my advantage over the years. I hope it demonstrates how simple it can be to take control of a situation by taking a chance. I get it can be scary to approach people (I'm still nervous most of the time!), but by knowing that you've got permission, are developing your confidence and have the right context, you'll find that it's enough to get you making far more connections than you ever thought possible.

To bring the Collision Code to life, whilst collisions and connections can happen without all three—permission, confidence and context—when combined (as you'll see from the stories) that's when the magic happens. The permission and confidence are ultimately about you. The context is the external factor, that enabler, the spark to the fire.

The Collision Code Framework

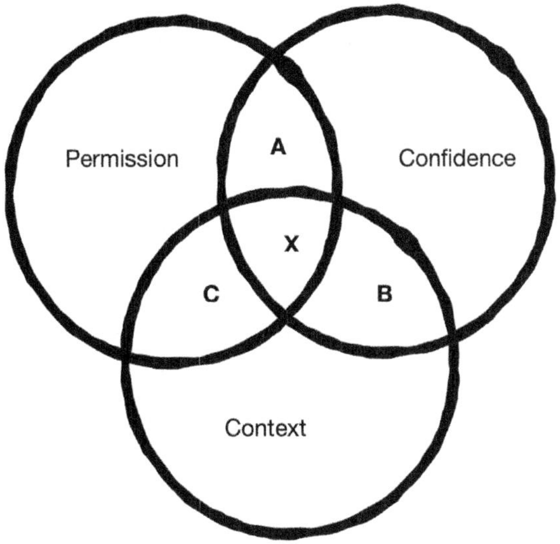
Permission
A
Confidence
X
C
B
Context

As you continue to read, I hope you'll see all the ways I've used this structure to my advantage over the years. On which note, let me continue the story.

Part I

Getting Going

First Steps

At school, it was my dream to work in the USA. I was fortunate enough to visit with family over the years (and have a mother with American heritage), and I was seduced by the sheer scale of everything, the immense opportunities on offer and the glamour. My dream in particular was to go to New York and so, after my A levels, I set my sights on getting to the Big Apple to undertake some work experience.

For the first part of 2001 I sent email after email, contacting firm after firm after firm (mostly in advertising, PR and marketing) to ask for a placement. It was a numbers game really, but it wasn't paying off. Those that did reply said I wasn't suitable or that I wouldn't be able to get the right visa as they couldn't sponsor me. It was frustrating. But never one to give up, I changed tack.

I found a company called Experience America that organised placements at businesses in San Francisco. It wasn't somewhere I'd dreamt about going, but since I was struggling to make any inroads in New York, I submitted an application. Within a few weeks, I had a placement at Gumps, a local retail icon right in the centre of downtown San Francisco, and I was ready to head Stateside.

I arrived in San Francisco in late August and stayed in a shared twin room with a desk under my bed. Most people who passed through were studying nearby, or learning English. It was a world away from England, but I liked it and I was determined to get stuck in.

My routine quickly took shape. Each morning I'd get ready and walk to work in the autumn sun, stopping to pick up a Starbucks on the way. Each day I got to know the staff a little better by asking questions and chatting as I waited and, before long, they were serving me a large hot chocolate, having only charged me for a small one. At eighteen years old this was my American dream!

I was the token intern with the British accent. I was in the corporate gifts and special events department. I felt like I was in a sitcom, the boss Brent overseeing everything. Aside from Brent, it was predominantly women, Danielle originally from Hawaii, Chloe, Jocelyn and Sandy. They all looked after me in their own way and took me under their wings. Sandy, like a typical Jewish grandmother, was ever so sweet, but she has sadly now passed away. I still have such fond memories of that time and have been back to visit and reconnect over the years.

Two weeks after arriving, terrorists flew two planes into the twin towers of the World Trade Center in New York. When

Part I Getting Going

I arrived at the office on 11 September, the news was reaching the world. I was told to head back home and wait for more information.

Back in my room, my roommate Zied was still asleep. I turned on the TV. The phones were down, or overloaded, so I couldn't speak to any family or friends. I managed to get to an internet cafe on the top floor of my accommodation to email home.

As the horror of that day unfolded, conversations in the building turned to whether it was safe to stay in San Francisco, or better to try to get back to our homes around the world. I didn't know, but I didn't feel that London would be any safer and so I made a decision to see out my time in the US. I carried on working at Gumps for a month or so, but things were difficult and people were being laid off, so I was assigned placements at both McCann Erickson and Sony Pictures Entertainment and a document sharing company called WorkShare. It was an unsettled time, but it was really informative to see how different kinds of businesses work.

When I was arranging the trip, I had booked my return to London from New York. I wasn't going to let the rejections get in the way of seeing the city. And I wasn't going to let terrorists have that control either. So, come October, I made my way to the East Coast to stay with friends of my father, his best man at his wedding, Tony and his wife Andrea.

On the plane after leaving San Francisco, I looked back at the emails I'd sent to all those companies in New York at the start of the year. Many of them were based in Lower Manhattan with some even in the towers. It was a mix of emotions. Life will throw those at you. As with everything, it's how you respond that counts.

I spent two weeks in New York at the end of October 2001. I noticed the dust on the bicycles still locked and unclaimed. Ground Zero remained cloaked in smoke and rubble.

As I flew back home I looked over the lights of the city that never sleeps, deeply humbled to have been welcomed so warmly by a community working its way to recovery.

Fate can be hard to fathom.

Reflection Time: What obstacles have you faced in pursuing your dreams, and how did you adapt to turn those challenges into opportunities for growth?

* * *

In December 2001 I got another job with a ski company. My plan was to spend the rest of the winter working in the mountains, while skiing as much as possible.

We headed by coach from Brighton to Montgenèvre in France, and I don't remember much about the first week beyond two things: copious amounts of alcohol, and the threat that if we didn't deliver, we'd be on the first coach back home.

I was assigned to a small ski resort called Le Corbier which was home to one British hotel. It wasn't glamorous work, but it was fun. A typical day would see me up at 7 a.m. to replenish the breakfast buffet and clear away dirty plates, before staff breakfast at 9 a.m. and then the rush to get a whole floor of rooms cleaned before lunch. After that our time was our own until 5 p.m. when we were fed before tending to the guests from 7 p.m. to 9.30 p.m. as they had their dinner.

I really enjoyed it. A good balance of hard graft and the opportunity for lots of skiing. As it happens I discovered I was really well suited to this kind of work. Not so much my cleaning or serving skills (much to the head chef's annoyance!), but when it came to customer service. Engaging with people and finding ways to go above and beyond was just something I did, and guests loved it as much as I did.

The Team Le Corbier 2002

The Collision Code

Every week I was fascinated by this slow burn process of turning strangers into friends. When anyone arrives they're just a name against a room number. When they appear in reception they are often tired, hungry and, sometimes literally given the weather, frosty. But over time as you help them, serve them, speak to them, drink with them, ski with them and make an effort to make their holiday as good as it can be, you become a kind of extended family. I was so proud at the end of the first week when my name was mentioned no less than fifteen times on the customer satisfaction surveys as someone who had made a difference. It was quite something to get even one mention. Did I get ribbed for it? I did. Did I care? Not a bit. I was just doing what I do and finding ways to be as helpful as I could (like the time the hotel ran out of ketchup and instead of telling guests, "No," I simply provided it from my own personal stash from my room).

The reality is this recognition simply came from being interested and caring. At that age, it can be seen as an uncool thing to do. I specifically even recall someone telling me they could do what I do, but they just couldn't be bothered! I'm not sure they understood what I was really doing. Being bothered is the key. Being available, being open, being kind, being proactive. And, of course, you often get far more back than you put in. Satisfaction, sure, but also bigger tips.

As the season wound on, the head office called to ask if I'd move to another resort a few hours away. Being a higher end hotel, the guests were particularly demanding, but it was actually a smaller hotel and a more flexible role which gave me more time to ski. It was also in Saint-Martin-de-Belleville, part of the Three Valleys which is one of the largest ski areas in Europe and still one of my favourite areas in the whole world. I was there, skiing every day and getting paid just by being me. Or, maybe more importantly, just by making the effort to be me.

That winter also helped me focus on how to start more conversations.

I remember sitting on the chairlifts day in, day out thinking, *I should say something to the person who happens to be sitting next to me.* After some trial and error, I soon hit upon a line that worked well every time: "Have you skied in the area recently?" It's disarmingly simple, and just requires a yes or no, but it could also lead to a much fuller conversation. Easy follow-ups like, "Where else have you been?" or "Where's been good?" came naturally, and nine times out of ten, the conversation flowed because of my confidence in asking, and the context of the ski lift. If it came up that I was skiing alone (the work rotas meant this was often the case), I was regularly invited to join my new friends for a few runs. I'm still in touch with some of the people I met on ski lifts.

The Collision Code

The great thing about a ski lift is it only lasts a few minutes. Long enough to see if there's a connection, but short enough that if it's awkward or someone doesn't want to talk, it doesn't really matter. That speed also forces you to just ask a question. It's amazing how freeing it is to have a "go-to" question that you can use without worrying, or wasting opportunities to connect with someone.

I always encourage people to think about situations you find yourself in often, where you might want to start a conversation, but aren't sure what to say. With a bit of thought and planning you can bypass the awkward tension and use something you prepared earlier when you had the time and space to consider what might work.

The best ice breakers are ones that allow people to give an open answer that can indicate how happy they are to talk to you.

- "What do you think of this place?"
  (Great for starting a conversation at a shared location, like a cafe, park or event.)
- "How did you discover this book/song/movie?"
  (This works well when noticing someone's interest in something specific.)
- "What's been the highlight of your day so far?"
  (This invites the person to share something positive and opens up the conversation.)

- "What brought you here today?"
  (This is useful in events, classes or social gatherings to understand someone's motivation.)
- "Have you been to any good restaurants/cafes/exhibitions/events lately?"
  (This can be a great conversation starter in a city or town.)
- "What are you doing this weekend? Or what do you wish you were doing?"
  (This question invites the person to share their interests and hobbies.)

And I know what you're thinking: "James, these sound like dodgy chat-up lines." I won't deny they could work that way, but only if that's your intent! If you simply want to have more conversations with people and see where they go, that's what it is. It's just a way to start a conversation, because if you don't start, you have nowhere else to go!

As an aside, the same thinking can also be really useful at events or presentations when the host asks if there are any questions. Often it can take a good minute or so for the room to warm up and for anyone to put their hand up. If you can be ready with a relevant question straight away, you can i) get an answer, and ii) become known to others in the room. This gives people context to talk to you afterwards ("I thought that was a really interesting question you asked earlier."). It works both ways.

It's a Numbers Game

After I finished my A levels, I took a year between school and university. To earn some money I did a short stint in telesales for Gala Bingo. My job was to phone people and offer them a free membership to Gala Bingo nationwide.

Out of 250 calls, I'd make maybe twenty-five "sales" each day, converting around ten percent. At the time I thought this was somewhat demoralising, but I've soon learnt it's actually a very good conversion rate. And whilst the money was useful to fund some travelling, the real value I got from that job was learning to deal with "no".

It taught me not to take "no" personally. People say no for all sorts of reasons, and it's almost never to do with you or how they feel about you. Experiencing literally hundreds of noes soon shakes off any concerns about making the offer, and by extension gives you the confidence to just do it, and move on.

Beyond that blunt reality check, it also taught me how to handle a no. I often refer to this experience as "no training" instead of sales training.

In the script we used, we were told to get a "no" three times before ending the call. This meant hearing "no" more than 700 times in a day. But that meant that, on occasion, someone who started out as a "no" became a "yes". Again, there's many reasons why someone might start as a no, then change their mind, and it's important to determine if it's a hard no, or just a reaction to being cold-called without really considering what's on offer. And while getting three noes may sound pushy, it's actually very easy to get there.

"Hi, my name is James. I'm calling from the Gala Bingo membership centre. I'm calling to offer you a free membership and a free gift. Would you be interested in that?"

"No, I'm not interested."

"Are you sure you're not interested in two chances every day to win £10,000 throughout May? It's completely free to sign up and I can just confirm a few details with you to get it done."

"It's not for me."

"OK, I hear you. All I need to do is confirm your postcode to get you signed up. There's a free gift as well, the food and drink is really well priced and you can also have up to six visitors with you on your membership..."

"No, thank you, as I say, I'm not interested."

And if it's another no, you can wish them a good day and move on. But you should see there's enough time there for someone to really consider if they want to hear more, or not. Of course, if they do stay on the line that's no guarantee of a sale, but if you walk away at the first no then you're definitely going to go without.

The Collision Code

As I've continued my own entrepreneurial journey, and particularly when I launched Student Beans (more on that later), I leant on all of this to get us off the ground. It really was the best sales training I could have had.

Sometimes I've found a "no" shifts the conversation and a totally different opportunity presents itself. But that only happens if you don't immediately shut down and move on. Generally people understand you're trying to promote your business or make another connection, so will accept a certain amount of tenacity. And as long as you're polite and move on when you've been given three noes, then you're unlikely to offend.

And, of course, this constant battering helped me build my confidence, one of those critical skills that would serve me so well in years to come.

Reflection Time: How can I reframe rejection in my life as an opportunity for growth rather than a setback?

* * *

Once actually at university, I quickly settled into life there. I never saw myself as an academic so it made sense for me to study business and that's exactly what I did, taking myself off to The University of Birmingham, excited for the next chapter of my life.

Shortly before the end of the first term, my friend Alex, a friend from London who happened to be in the same halls

Part I Getting Going

on the floor above, was chairing the committee organising the summer ball for our halls of residence and they needed someone to generate sponsorship for the event. It was a great opportunity for me, and one I had some idea how to tackle. By now, of course, I also knew that taking on the challenge would potentially lead somewhere interesting.

Having joined the committee I quickly set to work. I started by speaking to the manager of a small shopping complex in the centre of Birmingham. He was able to offer me some bags and, since there weren't quite enough to cover all the guests at the event, the local branch of United Colours of Benetton made up the numbers.

So I had some bags. Excited? I was. But maybe you're of the same mind as the committee who were less than impressed with my clutch of drawstring bags. Thing is, where they saw a limp bag, I saw an opportunity.

"What's going to go in the bag?"

"It's not a bag. It's a ball pack."

Their eyes rolled. "OK, James, what's going to go in the 'ball pack'?"

"Who knows. But now we have them, we have something to get sponsors excited about!"

They seemed less than enthused, so I made it my mission to make this work.

First, I created a list of potential sponsors and brands. Anyone that would appeal to students really: Pot Noodle, Durex, newspapers and so on. If I thought there was even a one percent chance of relevance and interest, they went on the list (Gala Bingo had taught me it really is a numbers game).

Then I started speaking to people.

At first I'd ask for paid sponsorship. Then, if the company said no, I'd ask for a sample or contribution to the goodie bags. If that failed, I asked if they'd be able to donate anything for the charity raffle.

Soon, my room was full of the most random stuff. Worm bookmarks from Waterstones, ground coffee from Starbucks, chocolate from Cadburys, Jelly Belly jellybeans, cinema tickets, pens and all the condoms Durex could send. Cafe Nero even gave us cups that people could redeem for a free hot drink. Businesses, when given something to consider, were really creative. Lush gave discount vouchers and some prizes for the raffle. My room smelt like one of their stores until I moved out!

STA Travel came on board to sponsor the ball tickets which was a great win. And then, in a stroke of real luck, it turned out the ball's theme, "the Oscars", gelled magnificently with Pot Noodle's new "Posh Noodle" range. This led to them sponsoring the whole event and doing some sampling on the night. We also had the local cinema put on a free screening for attendees, and a local club ran a pre-ball party. It was more than I could ever have hoped for.

Of course, not everything worked. I'd been keen to get Telewest (now part of Virgin Media) to offer free internet for a year to one house as a raffle prize thinking this would be a great promotion to 650 students about to move into rented accommodation for the first time, all needing internet. They didn't go for it, but a week before the ball I called one more time to say there was still time to include something in the raffle. The woman on the other end of the phone paused and then went to "look in the cupboard". They gave us an Xbox. Not sure why that made more sense to them, but it was a good prize.

I'd also had the idea to get *The Times* to provide newspapers for everyone to read over the breakfast that would be served at the event (it was a twenty-four-hour ball—students have plenty of energy!) *The Times* weren't interested so I contacted various other papers. It was the *News of the World* who liked the idea and delivered 650 copies in good time for breakfast karaoke.

Years later I was speaking about brand loyalty and happened to use a photo of everyone reading the newspapers over breakfast that morning. Afterwards an audience member came up to me. It turned out he was the person I'd contacted at *The Times* who had turned me down! He told me he'd liked the idea but hadn't been able to get sign-off internally.

So was it just a bag?

While it took a huge amount of persistence to get anywhere at all, the brands came through in droves and made the event really successful. If I had been scared of hearing no, we would have struggled to get anywhere. In developing a three-tiered approach—to ask for cash, items for goodie bags or raffle prizes—I found a way to make it easy for people to say yes to something. People, I think, generally want to say yes, it's just about finding something they (and other stakeholders) are comfortable with.

You can also, I hope, see how context played a huge role here. And how upfront, I created the permission for myself by deciding to make a real go of the sponsorship role which in turn gave myself permission to contact anyone and everyone. I also found the confidence grew with every small win, building on the foundations from all that time spent on the phone for Gala the year before.

I didn't know it at the time but I was going to spend a lot more time talking to brands about students. It's funny how you can sometimes pinpoint the origin of major life events, and how they felt just part of the process at the time.

AIESEC

In the first few weeks of university I learnt about AIESEC, a name originally drawn from *Association Internationale des Étudiants en Sciences Économiques et Commerciales,* and pronounced "eye-sek". It's the world's largest student-run organisation and it exists to develop the leaders of tomorrow, founded globally in 1948 after World War 2 with the idea of cultural understanding through exchange. If people go and live and work in another country, they'll not want to go to war against them—more relevant today than ever. It was founded in the UK in 1953 by Lionel Simons, an inspirational leader who created opportunities for many thousands of people over generations including myself.

My first encounter was in a busy lecture hall before a class. Two people walked in to make an announcement but, before saying anything else, simply asked for a volunteer. The room stayed quiet. I remember looking around, and others doing the same. *I could put my hand up,* I thought, *but what will they ask me to do?* There was a real nervous tension in the air as everyone pondered the same thing, fearing embarrassment if this was some kind of cruel stunt. After maybe sixty seconds the person sitting in front of me put their hand up and was invited down to the front.

His reward? A bottle of wine and an invitation to return to his seat. Life is, we were all told, about taking opportunities when they are presented. They introduced themselves as being from AIESEC and gave us details of an introductory talk if we wanted to learn more.

When the meeting rolled around I spoke to some friends in my halls asking them if they were interested in coming along. Everyone had an excuse, and I could have made one too. But I didn't.

Pitching up with Alex (the same friend who was chairing the summer ball committee), we found a seat at the front and listened intently to what they had to say. And then, having learnt more about AIESEC, we decided to apply for the programme. It's a competitive process, but that simply made it all the more appealing. As was clear, this was something for people who were willing to grab opportunities. I soon heard I'd been selected for the programme, and so had Alex.

What followed was life changing. I received training and development opportunities in sales, presenting, negotiation, recruitment and working with different cultures. This was all delivered by some of the many sponsors of AIESEC UK including but not exclusively PwC, KPMG, UBS, Cadbury Schweppes, DHL, Vodafone, the Tata Group, Procter & Gamble, and GSK.

We had exposure to many trainers but a special mention needs to go to Derek Small who provided the most incredible world-class leadership training including introducing me to Stephen Covey's work, author of *The Seven Habits of Highly Effective People*. Derek, I know, has been a huge supporter of AIESEC across the world. Over the last twenty years in business it's this training and similar trainings I've seen time and time again but the foundations started there. As students in AIESEC there really was no other opportunity like it.

I met Derek and his wife Maggie multiple times over a number of years. They kindly welcomed me into their home when I was working at the time in Wales when I was running Student Beans. Due to the rain there was flooding, the roads closed and trains were cancelled. I called them out of the blue and without hesitation they welcomed me in for the weekend with a comfy bed and home-cooked food. When I was diagnosed with my heart condition they extended an invite to visit them at their home in Spain which was a wonderful few days in the midst of adjusting to my new life. Derek also supported Michael, myself and the team at Student Beans with a number of leadership sessions which we really valued. I remember Derek saying, "It's the soft stuff that's the hard stuff." That's leadership. That's what so often isn't taught.

During my AIESEC experience I was also sent to the Philippines and Colombia. It was all paid for, or heavily subsidised, and led me to some incredible experiences and valuable connections. And all because I walked through a very welcoming open door.

The Philippines

Soon after I was accepted into AIESEC I applied for the Cultural Envoy for Exchange Development programme, aka CEED. It would see thirty people from across AIESEC UK travel abroad for six to ten weeks to help support AIESEC in a particular region by sharing knowledge from the UK. It was sponsored by HSBC who ran a similar exchange programme internally giving managers the opportunity to experience two-year placements around the world.

A key component of the programme was you didn't get to choose where you went. That didn't bother me. After all, the whole point of a proper cultural exchange is to be completely open no matter where you are.

I was placed in The Philippines, and originally planned to stay in one of the south islands. However, due to political unrest and resultant UK Foreign Office advice, it was decided I would stay in the capital, Manila.

Alex dropped me at the airport for my flight and left me with a parting gift: a book. I read it on the flight. The book, *The Naked Leader* by David Taylor, flipped my whole perception of the world. Among much else that resonated (which I will discuss in a later chapter) was a simple message: "Imagine if you couldn't fail. Who would you be? Where would you go? What would you do?" I didn't realise it until this point, but this was the lifestyle I'd been circling for years. I didn't have complete confidence in myself, and I was fuelled by nothing more than gut feeling, but this spoke to me intimately. I felt these words were written for me.

When I landed in Manila, my suitcase had not followed me. It wasn't ideal. All I had were the clothes on my back and a small bag. Fortunately I'd worn a suit jacket for the flight in a vain attempt to get an upgrade (which didn't work), so at least I looked smart for my initial meetings.

I was placed with a local AIESEC member in their home, staying in a spare room in an annexe outside the main house. I got the impression they weren't sure what to do with me, and the living arrangements somewhat reflected that. One morning I found a huge spider in the shower. I realised I had no idea if it was poisonous or not and what I should do, so I showed it to one of the maids working in the courtyard outside. She took off her slipper, slapped it and swept it up. Soon after I found a cockroach on top of the fridge. I paused. It seemed to look at me. Then it launched itself in my direction. It wasn't ideal. These were small things (the suitcase, the lack of structure, the bugs) but they weighed on me, and I wasn't sure this experience was for me after all.

Fortunately, I was able to find a safe haven in, of all places, Starbucks. A slice of normality (for me) just a few hundred yards from my accommodation. I would go there to hide in the corner, read and pretend I was somewhere else. It wasn't ideal, but it helped.

It was in Starbucks, one morning, that I read in the local paper about a Corporate Social Responsibility (CSR) event happening the next day. I asked around the AIESECers to see if anyone wanted to join me, but it was late notice and there were no takers. My entry in my journal for that day read, "I wonder what's going to happen tomorrow. I hope it all works out."

The next day I got up early and arrived at the venue well before anything started. I approached the information desk to buy a ticket for the event only to be told this wasn't possible. Gloria Macapagal Arroyo, president of The Philippines, was speaking and so, for security reasons, tickets were highly restricted.

Disappointed, I took myself round the open exhibition that formed part of the event, and tried to think of another way to get in. Looking at the agenda for the day I noticed that one of the speakers was Jaime Augusto Zobel de Ayala, CEO of the company that bears his name. Ayala is a huge Filipino company involved in everything from telecoms to retail and I knew they had a strong connection with AIESEC having sponsored many events over the years.

Having resolved to make the most of the day, I found context to speak to some people at the exhibition and soon found myself talking to a lady who worked for the Ayala Foundation. As we chatted she gestured over to Mr Ayala who had just walked in. I ended the conversation and set off like a man possessed. I don't really know what came over me, but in hindsight I suppose I knew that this was my one and only chance to salvage the day, and there was simply no option but to take it, or mope off home.

I asked if I could have a moment of his time.

He looked at me blankly.

I continued.

"Hi, I'm James, and I've just arrived from the UK as a representative of AIESEC. You have been a sponsor of some of our events I believe?"

He smiled. I told him I'd been keen to hear his keynote but hadn't realised I wouldn't be able to get a ticket today, and having just arrived had only just learnt the event was taking place. He must have liked my chutzpah because he turned to his assistant and after some conversation, I was registered, shuffled in and shown to one of the tables near the stage. It was me, and the heads of various Ayala corporation foundations.

Soon after settling down, the opening ceremony began with traditional dancing and a speech from the Filipino president. The rest of the agenda was filled with businesses talking about their activities in sustainability and CSR, including senior leaders from the World Development Bank and the head of HR from Shell.

The event was filled with food and drink, conversations and contacts. It was marvellous, and the next day I decided I would return. I realised I still didn't have official status, but at this point I wasn't going to let that stop me. I showed my day-one pass to security and somehow convinced them to let me in with that. I don't think anyone actually thought to question it. So I did the same on day three. It was a hugely rewarding and interesting few days and it put me in a position to make the most of my stay in The Philippines (a trip in which I also narrowly avoided a military coup, witnessed a bank robbery and travelled throughout the country... but those are for another book!)

I haven't spoken to Jaime Augusto Zobel de Ayala since, but it's amazing what can happen when you decide to do what you would do if you knew you couldn't fail. AIESEC gave me the excuse (i.e. the context) to speak to anyone so much more than simply saying I was a student.

Colombia

I'd applied, without success, for a leadership role in the AIESEC Birmingham chapter, but was invited instead to take on the position of Vice President of Outgoing Exchange. I would be responsible for running a team and recruiting students to send them abroad. Up until now my experiences with AIESEC had been local, finding placements for international graduates in and around Birmingham. This was a new experience entirely.

I'd recently taken on a role as brand manager for Yell.com for Birmingham and wasn't sure if I had the time to do both. But I'd also just discovered I'd be going to The Philippines and thought that I'd regret it if I turned down the chance to get more involved. After some deliberation and conversations with the national team, including Andrea Elliot, the National Vice President of Outgoing Exchange, I bit the bullet and said yes.

It was a great decision, as when I returned from Manila I was absolutely driven to make the most of the coming year.

First, I recruited a team to help me. This itself was really rewarding, as I was able to see the journey the team went on in the course of the year. At the start some couldn't even speak in front of an audience, and by the end they were running the whole process. It's often said that leadership isn't really about you, it's about how many other leaders you're able to create. This was a really rewarding example.

During that year I worked closely with Andrea and, on one visit to AIESEC's UK office, she told me that a participant in that year's "Pioneer" programme had dropped out. It was a programme I had applied for, but been unsuccessful as it offered an opportunity to live and work in Colombia. She asked if I wanted the place and, of course, I said yes. It's funny how things come about in the end if you just keep going.

Before leaving I had the idea to contact the BBC in Birmingham to suggest that those students travelling over the summer could share their stories on the local news portal. Our contact there, Suzanne, was brilliant and we arranged to have four students share their adventures from Colombia, the Czech Republic, India and the Philippines. Our diaries are still live online at:

https://bit.ly/jebbcbirmingham

And so, in July 2004, I packed up and headed to Barranquilla on Colombia's Caribbean coast.

At the airport I was met by Juan Mulford whose family I would be staying with. We soon learnt we were born on exactly the same day—a fine coincidence—and so began the most enjoyable time spent in their company. The family was amazing, embracing me as one of their own. I lived in their home with them generously providing amazing food and kind hospitality. It was really an incredibly humbling experience.

During the week I worked for an organisation called the Costa Atlantica Project. It is a pre-school education programme designed to bring people together by socialising children from neighbouring communities that were traditionally in conflict with each other. It is hoped that by forging friendships among young people barriers can be broken down and tension relieved.

Dealing with this sensitive topic as an outsider, especially with the language barrier, was tough, but with Google Translate and the help of others I muddled through.

As in The Philippines, immersion in the whole culture was a key part of the experience. On weekends we would explore as best we could, but Colombia remained in some turmoil with many trips inland forbidden to tourists due to the heightened potential for kidnappings. It was a different time then back in 2004. But we made the most of what we had, exploring the beautiful Tayrona National Park and its incredible rainforest that meets the Caribbean Sea. We hiked, we swam, we drank, we sang and enjoyed an incredible few days with friends new and old. It was bliss.

On the way back, the sun had just ducked under the horizon and the bus stopped at a checkpoint. An official asked everyone to show identification. I hadn't brought my passport on the trip, but I did have my driving licence. This turned out to be a problem.

Another traveller and I were asked to leave the coach. All advice at the time said not to engage with the police if at all possible. This was partly due to corruption, but also due to gangs masquerading as the police to give a premise for isolating and kidnapping individuals in hope of a ransom. I looked at Dan, who was with me on the Pioneers programme, and pleaded for him to join me.

We walked slowly down the coach. I didn't want to get off, but a man with a rifle is hard to argue with. Even more so when you don't speak the language.

Dan explained, in Spanish, that I was sorry I didn't have my passport but that a driving licence is official documentation. He showed both his licence and his own passport to the guards.

After some more hushed discussion, they let us return to our seats. After a few minutes the other traveller was allowed back on the bus as well, and we were on our way. It was overwhelming and frightening and I was very glad that Dan was there.

At the end of that summer I returned back to the UK so grateful to AIESEC and those I had met on the trip. Andrea and I kept in touch over the years and I visited her while she was working in the Hague. We chatted often when she returned to the UK, though never managed to find time to meet up.

The next time I saw her was at the AIESEC UK Sixtieth Celebration black-tie dinner. We shared a cab home as she was now living in the same part of town. It was the last time I saw her. Not long after that night, she was visiting Ireland with her fiancé and they were involved in a car accident. Both died at the scene. I attended her cremation and I think of her often. She was a special person, full of life and she supported and believed in me. She is much missed.

You don't know when you're going to go.

Or when someone you love or admire will.

The only thing you can count on is now.

If you have something to say, or something to do, please don't delay.

Inspired by my experiences with AIESEC, and wanting to give back, the Elliott International Opportunity Fund was created in memory of Andrea in July 2023. I set it up including a donation with another AIESEC alumni to provide an opportunity for AIESEC UK members to go abroad. In its first year, over twenty young people benefited from the programme. I hope this is a legacy that will continue for many years to come.

* * *

AIESEC was such a huge part of my life at university. At just nineteen years old I was able to tell people, without any exaggeration, that I was a regional development business manager. I travelled the world and I met incredible people.

In Colombia I found a resource pack that had been put together by James Shaw, an AIESECer from New Zealand. It was so helpful that I contacted James to say thank you and it turned out he was based in London. When I returned, we met up.

The Collision Code

Later, when I was running Student Beans (more on that later), James introduced me to another New Zealand AIESECer, Dave Clearwater. Dave was working for Milkround, the graduate recruitment company, and James thought it would be a helpful connection. He was right. Dave introduced me to Tom Hughes, the founder of Milkround, which provided some incredible opportunities to Student Beans amounting to tens of thousands of pounds of business. It was a great chain of events.

I've also regularly been invited to speak at events as an AIESEC alumnus. At one of these, in Portugal, I met Majken, originally from Denmark. Years later, and totally by chance, I bumped into her in London to find out she was living just round the corner. We met up a few times and it was through her partner, Emanuel, that I discovered The Marketing Academy (more on *that* later too—can you see a theme?).

And then there was Sammie.

Sammie came to the UK as a graduate from Kenya to take part in the AIESEC exchange programme which I was running. After the university summer ball, I had built a number of connections, one of which was AMC Theatres. The manager of their brand-new local multiplex cinema, Damian Drabble, was my contact and during one of our conversations he highlighted he was looking for someone to handle marketing. I explained about AIESEC's programme and he loved the idea. He paid the exchange fee and we set about finding the right person. That person was Sammie.

Later on Sammie and AMC came back into my lives when I was launching Student Beans in Birmingham and Manchester. They devised a two-for-one cinema ticket for students that meant two people could go to a film for just £3. Even in 2005 that was a bargain. I still meet people today who remember that offer!

It's amazing how AIESEC gave me the context to have so many conversations with people, not just once, but over and over again. It gave me something interesting to share, and it plugged me into a network that always had something new to offer.

I always advise people to look back at friendships from yesteryear, or contacts that have drifted away. Everyone you don't keep in touch with is a lost opportunity, so think of ways to rekindle that. Not to sell or self-promote, of course, but just because it's of value in itself. You don't know where things will lead, and things don't matter just because they lead somewhere. But without connections, it's hard to find yourself in new and unexpected places. And that's where you begin to thrive.

Being student focused, as I entered my final year of university I knew my time with AIESEC was winding up. There was, however, one more thing I was desperate to do: hold a role on the national team. The opportunity to be elected was each January, and I felt I was ready.

The way I saw it, AIESEC had invested a huge amount of time and money in me, and I was ready to give back. I'd travelled, I'd been given a platform, I'd learnt skills I'd use forever, I'd been able to test and learn and fail and then find ways to succeed. I was so passionate about the organisation I just wanted to help others have what I'd had.

Elections were being hosted in a hotel in Walsall, not far from Birmingham. As part of the process each candidate had to give an opening speech, sit on a Q&A panel, give an impromptu talk on a subject revealed just thirty minutes in advance, and then give a closing speech. They were long days and there was a huge amount going on. Everyone, of course, had their own ideas and expectations and it was hard to escape the edge of relentless competition at every turn, even if everyone was ultimately very friendly.

The president was elected on Friday, the second day of the conference. The elections for vice presidents—for which I was standing—came during the last session on Sunday. In total five places were available, with nine of us looking to succeed.

As we shuffled onto the stage to hear the results, there was no more to do except look out at 250 people, and hope. There's an odd tradition in these elections whereby successful candidates have a jug of water poured over their head (don't ask). This means if you stay dry, you've been unsuccessful, though at least you don't have to get changed. Decisions made, we awaited our fate. The outgoing team lined up behind us. A drum roll blasted through the room. People clapped, people stomped, people hollered. And the jugs were raised high...

For me, time stood still. I could see the AIESEC Birmingham delegates who'd been so supportive looking up at me in disbelief. I hadn't been selected. To say I was upset doesn't cover it. I was absolutely bereft.

Sometimes we experience failure without any fanfare. The job rejection opened in private we can convince ourselves, and others, we didn't want anyway, for example. But this was very public. There was no hiding how much I'd wanted this role. Over the days and weeks that followed I really struggled to process what had happened. As far as I was concerned I was the best person for the job, but it wasn't to be.

I explored opportunities with the national teams in Sweden, Dubai and Ireland but didn't get very far. And so, with that, my time with AIESEC was up.

Except, of course, as I demonstrated above, it wasn't. The experience lives on. The connections live on. The months and years of time spent learning and developing and discovering made it possible for me to become the person I am today. Failure exists, of course, and indeed it can hurt, but you have to put it in perspective. It is only by coming up against obstacles and finding ways to get around them that we discover who we really are.

Reflection Time: In what ways can your own experiences of stepping outside your comfort zone and embracing opportunities shape your future decisions and personal growth?

Diageo

It was the beginning of my final year at university and I knew I wanted to do my dissertation on coaching and its impact in organisations. While attending an information session with Diageo, the drinks company behind Johnnie Walker, Archers, Bailey's and other household names, I approached the speaker at the end of the evening. My plan was to get her details to try to secure a conversation with someone in the HR department about how they use coaching. I emailed the next morning and, a few days later, received a call from a person called Emma Rees. I shared that I was looking to interview some of the team who'd received coaching and, much to my surprise, she invited me to attend their in-house high performance coaching programme. The course was due to be held in Milton Keynes over two days and overnight—all I had to do was turn up and they could cover the costs. I couldn't believe my luck and jumped at the opportunity.

The date of the course arrived and I met initially with Terry Murphy and Emma, the two facilitators. As the programme properly began, there was an introductory session where we were paired up and had to introduce each other to the room. As part of this we were to choose three key life moments that led us to where we were today. Over the next few days we went into the depths and structure of coaching and various models that are used. That evening we went bowling and out for dinner. It was all a wonderful experience and I felt so lucky that I had been welcomed and felt part of the team. I was actively encouraged to share and contribute and I interviewed everyone who attended the course over the two days.

At the end of the programme I went to my car and got a couple of books to say thank you to the facilitators. One of them was *The Naked Leader*. The other was *Change the World for a Fiver* written by Eugénie Harvey who I had the pleasure to meet a couple of times over the years. The book is all about simple tangible things that you can do to change the world, very much ahead of its time and still applicable today including saying no to plastic bags, doing double-sided photocopying and instead of using disposable cups have a reusable mug. I was hugely inspired by this book and its message—small actions can change the world, one action at a time.

I followed up with an email after thanking them and was blown away by the response:

From: Murphy, Terry
Subject: RE: Thank You
Date: 19 November 2004 at 12:37:30 GMT
To: James Eder, Emma Rees
Cc: Terry Murphy

James,

Before I met you I had a perception of you and why you wanted to work with us. What a wonderfully sad thing paradigms are until we break out of them.

You are a truly live and inspirational example of "be the change you want to see in the world" and as such, although you may say you would have liked to have met Gandhi, I'm sure he would say that you are following in his sandal marks.

I have in the past been a stuck-in-the-mud corporate animal but have found that the role I currently have allows me to break away from this and help others to push the boundaries and think of things differently. You, however, go way beyond this and have helped me to make a further step change in this wonderful journey called life.

I'm smiling more! I'm achieving more! I'm hugging more! I'm refusing plastic carrier bags! I've committed to taking my mug to work! I turn off lights and watch less TV! I'm reading more stories to the kids and will plant my Xmas tree seeds! I've started double-sided photocopying!

I will not, however, give my book **Change the World For a Fiver** to anyone as it will stay with me to remind me of a young man *with a rather large brain who has the ability and energy to make a difference!! But I will go and buy ten copies and pass them round Diageo... if this has the same impact on others then very soon this book will be in every house in the country.*

Not often am I moved to such feedback which is heartful and sincere but probably not to HPC criteria.

You are an inspiration and a new gem that the world needs!

"Be the change..."

Kindest regards,

Terry.

I followed up a number of months later interviewing the key stakeholders on the impact of the programme to round off my research. In the end I received a 2:1 for the dissertation and it laid the foundations and groundwork that enabled me to be a better leader and manager, and later to pursue my own practice as a coach. I am forever grateful to Diageo, Terry and Emma for being so welcoming and supporting me.

Reflection Time: Reflecting on your own journey, what opportunities have you embraced that have significantly impacted your personal or professional development, and how can you continue to seek and maximise such opportunities in the future?

The London Innovation Conference

Towards the end of my university experience in 2005, I read about an event called The London Innovation Conference. The tickets were priced in the hundreds of pounds—far beyond what I could afford at the time—so I decided to contact the organisers. I introduced them to AIESEC and asked whether they might be willing to provide us with some tickets. To my surprise, they responded and offered me tickets for just £25! I gathered a delegation of five from Birmingham, and the day was fantastic. Almost twenty years later, I still remember some of the speeches and the lessons I learnt.

One of the key moments was my first exposure to Lord Bilimoria, best known as the founder of Cobra Beer. His journey resonated deeply with me, especially as I was about to launch Student Beans. He spoke about going door-to-door to get Cobra Beer into restaurants, a process that mirrored my own experience of pitching Student Beans to potential partners. He shared insights into the thought behind bottle design, the storytelling aspect of branding, and the resilience, persistence and drive needed to build a successful business. Over the years, we've crossed paths at various events, including at the House of Lords, and through his involvement with the University of Birmingham Business School, where he also served as Chancellor.

Another inspiring speaker was Sahar Hashemi OBE, who spoke about her journey in co-founding Coffee Republic with her brother, Bobby. This resonated with me as I was preparing to start my own business with my brother. One phrase she shared has stayed with me ever since:

> "If you jump, a net will appear."

So often, I find myself hesitating over whether to take action or not, and this quote comes to mind. More often than not, we don't know exactly how things will unfold—but we need to trust that it will work out. As my journey has continued, I've seen the power of this mindset. No matter how daunting something seems, a net will appear. Recently, someone shared another piece of wisdom with me:

> "Everything will work out in the end. If it hasn't worked out, it isn't the end."

It's all too easy to stay in our comfort zones—whether that's avoiding risks or even something as simple as not saying hello to someone when we feel we should. But real growth happens when we step outside that comfort zone, even if it feels uncomfortable at first.

One of the other keynote speakers that day was Gary Beckwith, the founder of City Cruises. After hearing him speak, I reached out to him, and a few months into my first year of running the business, he agreed to meet with me. He shared three key lessons that I often find myself passing on to clients and contacts when discussing business challenges. I wanted to share them here:

1. There can only be one captain of the ship. This particularly resonated with me as I had co-founded Student Beans with my brother, Michael. Early on, challenges emerged because we hadn't clearly defined who was the "captain". Over time, we refined our roles—Michael as Operations Director, focusing internally, and me as Commercial Director, focusing externally. Once our roles were clearer, communication improved significantly. When I stepped away from the day-to-day business after ten years, it allowed Michael to step into the role of Managing Director and CEO, bringing even greater clarity to the organisation. Having one clear leader makes a huge difference.

2. Someone needs to be responsible for making sure there's always a spare ink cartridge. This simple analogy highlights the importance of clearly defined responsibilities within a business. It's not just about assigning tasks—it's about thinking ahead. It's the difference between someone being responsible for ordering ink cartridges and ensuring that if the ink runs out, a replacement is already there. That level of forward-thinking and accountability can have a huge impact on an organisation.

3. We always have a choice. At the time, Student Beans was only operating in Birmingham, but we were preparing to expand to eighteen cities. This decision was largely driven by feedback from brands who told us they would only work with us if we had national coverage. It felt like we had no choice. But looking back, I realise the power of feeling in control. When you actively choose your path—rather than feeling pushed by external pressures—it creates a sense of empowerment and ownership that is invaluable.

Conferences are a brilliant opportunity to learn, grow and be inspired. They provide the chance to connect with like-minded people, meet interesting speakers and build your network. The atmosphere of a conference can spark new ideas and fuel your passion.

Reflection Time: What events or conferences could you attend to inspire you and connect with like-minded people?

The Naked Leader

You might recall that before a flight to The Philippines, my friend Alex handed me a book called *The Naked Leader*. Before that point I'd never heard of the author, David Taylor, but I trusted Alex's judgement. I started reading the book on the flight with no real expectations and found it to be an easy read of forty-two short stories wrapped around seven different themes. I read it straight through in one go.

David Taylor keeps things simple and acknowledges that most business and personal development books are never actually read through. On this basis he gives his "answer" right at the start of the book, and it's the lesson I shared with you previously: "Imagine if you couldn't fail. Who would you be? Where would you go? What would you do?"

The Collision Code

I've always found there to be a huge amount of hype and jargon around the concept of leadership, which is why *The Naked Leader*'s stripped back and fundamental approach really resonated with me. Another line I took from the book that stuck with me was, "Be the leader you already are." This idea that you already have everything you need, you just have to believe it and approach things with that perspective really resonated with me.

Throughout my trip to The Philippines I kept thinking about the content of the book. And so, when I returned, I wrote to David and asked if he'd be willing to meet me.

He said yes (though he later told me he wasn't initially going to agree, but decided on a whim "why not"—sometimes it takes the right moment!)

I was keen to speak to David about AIESEC and to see if there was a way to involve him, and I wanted to thank him for writing such a transformational book. I remember I put together a PowerPoint presentation with slides to guide the conversation, but he immediately told me just to speak from the heart. So I did. At the end of the meeting he said he'd be interested in getting involved in some capacity and we agreed to work out what later. I wanted to get him to speak at one of our conferences, but was just pleased he was interested at all.

As my studies continued, we hadn't talked further, but I remained on David's mailing list and noticed that he was coming to London to speak. I bought a ticket and made the trip down for the day.

At the event David, of course, told the audience to believe that they couldn't fail. And so, taking his advice yet again, I strode up to him at the end of the event.

"David, hello. You've always told me to imagine what I'd do if I couldn't fail. So here I am putting it into practice and asking you to speak at an AIESEC event." There was a short pause. I wondered what he was thinking, hoping I'd approached it the right way. After a moment he smiled and agreed we'd find a way to make it work.

Sometimes, maybe all the time, you just have to ask plainly. After all, a vague notional commitment to do something one day is not the same as a firm, specific commitment.

I introduced David to the coordinator of AIESEC's National Conference with the aim of getting him to speak that year to around 200 students from across the UK. Unfortunately the theme and programming didn't really work, so the plan was made for him to speak at the National Conference in 2005.

Fast forward to the conference and I was invited to host David's session, which was just as awe-inspiring for all 200 attendees as I'd hoped. It's such a rewarding thing to see a room of people totally motivated and inspired by the simple idea that anything is possible, and really believing it. David delivered more than I'd ever wished for, and everyone agreed it was a huge success. I was very grateful.

Before David headed off, we sat down and talked. I told him I'd recently failed to get onto the AIESEC national team. As I put it to him, I'd imagined I couldn't fail, but it turned out I could!

David asked if there was anything he could do to help. At that stage, there wasn't. But then he turned the tables on me.

"What did being on the national team really mean to you? Is there a way you can achieve everything you'd hoped to do with AIESEC through another channel?" Failure, after all, cannot exist with persistence.

While I had failed in that moment in that particular context, the aspiration was very much there: to be able to help students, to make a difference and provide opportunities for them; to challenge myself; to not be a cog in a big machine; and to take things from idea to reality. Could I achieve all those things another way? Of course.

It was in that moment of reframing that Student Beans really blossomed into life. It became not just an idea, but my only option. And if I imagined that Student Beans couldn't fail, what was I waiting for?

Friends and elders around me suggested I was too young to start a company. I reasoned, however, that being a student-focused company, being closer to that cohort gave me an edge. Everything else I'd work out. My parents were hugely supportive which helped; somehow they knew this was what I was meant to do.

Over the years David and I have stayed in touch and I've been a big advocate for his message. For many, it's the fear of failure that stops them starting in the first place. But don't be that person. I'm glad I wasn't, and David is to thank for that. I've hoped for many years now that by sharing this story, I can inspire at least one other person to make a leap they might otherwise have been too scared to make. Maybe that's you?

Reflection Time: How can you reframe your own experiences of perceived failure to uncover new opportunities and paths for growth, and what steps will you take to pursue those possibilities with confidence?

Student Beans

When I started university, a close friend asked me a simple question, "Why are you going?"

As you've read, before getting to Birmingham University, I'd had this incredible year working and travelling, and before that my experience launching needanumber.co.uk which had given me a taste for entrepreneurship. Indeed, just when I was closing down needanumber, some people were saying I should be doing the opposite. "Sack off uni!

Focus on building this startup!" I ultimately chose the less shaky path of A levels and university, but, of course, part of me always wondered what would have happened if I'd stuck with it. Especially as more and more tech startups, some not dissimilar, ballooned and made millionaires and billionaires around the world.

But that time had passed, and so I was at university, and I was able to answer that simple question by pointing to the sackful of opportunities and new experiences I was afforded: living in halls, organising the summer ball, being brand manager for Yell.com, joining AIESEC and all that entailed with placements in The Philippines and Colombia and even a degree in there too. All of which gave me the tools to feel more confident in pursuing a less well-worn path when the opportunity next presented itself.

Part of my degree involved writing a business plan. Every student could pick whatever they wanted, but I was very clear from the beginning what my focus would be. All my experiences had led me to realise there was a real market for connecting brands with students and offering those students deals and discounts.

The first incarnation of what would become Student Beans was in that original business plan back in 2004. I'd envisaged a website that students would log on to in order to print discount vouchers to take into shops and other businesses, initially in Birmingham, but with a view to expanding. I mentioned this to my older brother, Michael, and he perked up. Normally he'd tell me my business ideas were terrible, but this was different. He thought there was something there, and having worked briefly for JP Morgan in investment banking before becoming a titanium power-seller (it's as impressive as it sounds!) on eBay, I trusted his judgement. Indeed, it was Michael who came up with the name "Student Beans", noting the British student staple of baked beans mirrored the "staple" of student lives we wished to become.

Whilst the business plan was in its first incarnation I had read in the news that Apax, a leading global private equity advisory firm, had acquired Yell.com and all its assets. Following the format, I guessed the email address of one of the partners who had worked on the deal, Stephen Grabiner, and sent an email with the context that I was a Yell.com brand manager at the University of Birmingham and that I was working on a few business ideas and would he meet with me. He agreed to meet and I shared my various business ideas including the idea for an oxygen bar that I'd seen whilst in San Francisco. He veered me away from that one but suggested the student discount platform had legs.

He knew Humphrey Black who by chance had worked on launching Virginstudent.com an internet startup funded by Virgin. It was a social networking startup for UK university students, five years before Facebook. An introduction was made and it was an amazing opportunity to get feedback from him on the initial concept and business plan.

Michael, 'The Bean' & James

By this point, it was a "we". Michael was keen to get involved and really bring this thing to life. After finishing the business plan, I juggled the rest of my studies before graduation with going door to door trying to sell the idea to businesses.

The business was officially registered at Student Beans Ltd on 21 June 2005 with Michael and I owning fifty percent each.

One of the first things we did was sit down, separately, to write out our vision for the business. I was amazed, and relieved, that they were strikingly similar. We both brought our own skills and approach to the business (myself in sales and marketing, Michael in operations) and quickly found our own roles day to day. I hope to write more about the Student Beans journey in another book, but there are some experiences I think are worth sharing here…

* * *

I was waiting for a lecture at the University of Birmingham Business School, when I spotted Dave Lewis from The Prince's Trust standing behind a stall. The Prince's Trust was founded in 1976, by His Majesty King Charles III, when he was His Royal Highness The Prince of Wales. Having completed his duty in the Royal Navy, His Majesty became dedicated to improving the lives of disadvantaged young people in the UK. He founded The Prince's Trust to deliver on that commitment.

By this point Student Beans was already starting to happen, and we talked about the support that might be available for the fledgling business. However, I had already set up a meeting with the bank to discuss a business loan, so it wasn't something I thought we needed.

Of course, I soon learnt that the course of business rarely runs smoothly. The manager at the bank who'd normally deal with our application was off sick, and so a junior staff member met with me and dismissed the application immediately on the basis it was a website. Frustrated, but not willing to give up, I got in touch with Dave and talked him through our business plan. When I told him what happened at the bank he told me that if I could get an official "rejection letter" I would be eligible for a low-interest loan from The Prince's Trust. When one door shuts...

Letter received and application made, we were soon awarded a £3,000 loan, which went straight into web development, but that wasn't the end of the relationship. Over the coming months we were given business mentors from DLA Piper, the law firm, Emily Aviss and Mark Beardmore. We had monthly meetings on legal and financial matters which was so helpful in holding us properly accountable and keeping us focused.

It was even more helpful when, a few weeks into the life of Student Beans, we found someone copying all our work! Another website was literally scraping our content, images and even the logos of brands I had personally scanned in and created. Thankfully with the right relationships, we were able to get a proper "cease and desist" letter drafted and sent to the offending party, which worked.

The Prince's Trust, now known as The King's Trust, does fantastic work, over the years impacting and helping over a million young people. I am forever grateful for their support at the beginning of my entrepreneurial journey. Have those conversations and hold onto those connections. They can be the thing that will help you turn it around when you start to struggle. Twenty years on I'm proud to be a member of part of their Enterprise Network, a group of people giving back to The King's Trust and helping to support the next generation of young people and entrepreneurs.

Connections Continue To Give

There are some very special people who believed in us from the very beginning. One such person was Victoria from Best Imports. I'd first spoken to her when I'd looked to get Jelly Belly jellybeans into the summer ball packs in my first year at university (they were responsible for the UK distribution). Victoria was the PR manager and she was able to get us some boxes of jellybeans for the ball packs, for which I was most grateful.

I'd been obsessed with Jelly Belly as a brand for years. I used to go to Selfridges in London to stare at the display of all the flavours when I was a kid. It just mesmerised me. In my final year at university, one of the modules asked us to create a presentation on a successful brand. I convinced my group that the brand should be Jelly Belly.

In the lead up I contacted Victoria again, and she was wonderful, delivering us T-shirts to wear in the presentation, as well as samples, menus, leaflets and more. We went to town on the presentation with her help and were awarded a first for the project. We also shared it with Jelly Belly afterwards, and Victoria said it was the best she'd seen during her twenty years in the role. That was such a boost.

At this point Student Beans wasn't even a concept. Yet, this relationship provided me with a perfect "in" when I most needed to convince brands to get on board with our vision. And, of course, the "bean" connection was tailor-made! Having talked to Victoria through a haze of excitement, she agreed to provide us with 10,000 samples for our launch. And this was just the start.

Over the years we have collaborated on sampling promotions, attended all our meetings with a jar of Jelly Belly product to leave with prospective and current clients, and I'd even give out beans with my bean-shaped business card.

It was such a joyful partnership, and I'm so grateful to Victoria for believing in me and our team, and for all of Best Imports for being so supportive over the years. I still meet people almost twenty years on who remember me bringing Jelly Belly to their offices.

Victoria taught me to assume that every relationship will go somewhere, and to nurture and treasure them for some point in the future. Because even if they don't, it's a much more positive way to go about business.

* * *

Over the years at Student Beans, there were many notable moments that utilised The Collision Code, but there are just a couple more I feel are worth mentioning here.

One example is Krispy Kreme, another iconic American brand. They had launched one of their early concessions in Selfridges at the Bullring in Birmingham city centre. Instead of charging them a listing fee on Student Beans, we struck a deal: they provided a special discount of "Buy one dozen, get one dozen free" in exchange for one hundred dozen doughnuts, which we used as prizes for a promotion.

When we launched the website in Birmingham, I personally went door to door in Selly Oak—the main student area—knocking on student houses and handing out window stickers. I told students that if they put the sticker up, they had a chance to win a prize for their house if they were spotted by the "Bean Patrol."

Later that academic year, during exam season, I drove to Krispy Kreme, loaded my car with the boxes of doughnuts, and delivered them to the lucky winners—students whose houses displayed the Student Beans logo stickers and were randomly selected. It was such a buzz! I even received messages from friends in other cities talking about the giveaway.

Another incredible partnership was with The Accor Group, the owner of Etap, which was later rebranded and incorporated into the Ibis Budget brand.

One of the biggest challenges of running a non-funded startup is keeping costs down, and as we expanded into different cities, one of my main concerns was finding affordable accommodation. So, I walked into the local Etap hotel in Birmingham city centre and explained my situation to the manager. Incredibly, they agreed to provide £5,000 worth of hotel stays in exchange for the equivalent value in advertising.

This partnership was a game-changer. It allowed me to travel the country and stay at any of their hotels while launching in new cities. If there wasn't a budget hotel nearby, I could even stay in a Novotel—one of their more premium brands. Not only did this cover the room, but it also included bed and breakfast. During the scorching summer of 2006, as I traveled to a new city each week, having air-conditioned rooms and city-centre parking made a huge difference.

This experience reinforced an important lesson: business is built on relationships. Behind every brand, it's individuals who make the difference. And it's individuals like this who help startups succeed—one hotel night at a time.

* * *

Nesta is a UK-based organisation focused on innovation. In early 2006 I was at one of their networking events attended by entrepreneurs from around the country where I met Paul Birch the co-founder of Bebo, one of the first big social networks. I told him about Student Beans, and sensing a fellow technical founder, he asked me what language the website was in.

"English?" I said, somewhat naively.

He wrapped up the conversation at that point, but did suggest I meet with a few people he knew including Michael Acton Smith entrepreneur and co-founder of Calm, who at the time was working on MindCandy, the business behind Moshi Monsters (an interactive games company). As the conversation continued, the consensus seemed to be that this was never going to work because, as a two sided-market place, it would be stuck in the classic chicken and egg rut. No students, because no discounts, but no discounts, because no students. The thing is, I left those conversations more motivated than ever to succeed. And also to find out what programming language the website was written in (PHP, for the record).

I don't know why it inspired me so much. I certainly respected these opinions and I understood their point, but I knew from my experience in this particular area that the brands wanted this, and so did the students. It wasn't going to be easy, sure, but there was a successful business here and I was going to make it happen.

* * *

At the beginning, Student Beans was just a holding page with "coming soon" in big letters, and I was a wide-eyed founder networking like crazy to try to find the people who would help us bring it to life. One event I went to was at

BNI (Business Networking International) where I met another Victoria who worked at a law firm. While she couldn't help, she did introduce me to Pom who had recently joined KPMG in the Learning and Development team and we met up.

At the time Pom hadn't even started her new role, but we stayed in touch and I was thrilled when she agreed to buy some advertising space on the website in five UK regions. We came up with a price of £3,000 as a starting point, but KPMG wanted exclusivity. We thought it over and proposed £7,000, which they took.

It was by far the biggest deal we'd done at that point and, as well as the cash, just having such a large and well-known brand on board made it so much easier to have subsequent conversations with new prospects.

I remember Pom reminding me that, despite the size of KPMG, people do business with people. It is always the individual connections that will make things happen. And even when someone can't help, like Victoria, they might just know someone who can. Everyone is a potential collaborator in some way or form.

Reflection Time: How can you leverage your existing connections and experiences to create new opportunities in your own life, and what steps will you take to nurture those relationships for future growth?

Part 1 Getting Going

Start-Up Loans

As my profile had grown with Student Beans, back in 2012, I was invited to be one of the twelve original ambassadors for The Start-Up Loans Company. It was Lord Young's conception and James Cann was founder and chairman of the government-funded scheme to provide advice, business loans and mentoring to startup businesses from across the UK.

We were all young entrepreneurs who had set up their businesses with less than £3,000. We supported the launch of Start-Up Loans by being examples of what you can achieve on limited start-up capital. The twelve ambassadors included Carrie Green of the Female Entrepreneur Association, Jodie Cook who at the time was running JC Social Media and Richard Hurtley of Rampant Sporting.

At the first meeting of the original ambassadors, James Caan, Bev James and Duncan Cheatle greeted the ambassadors in London at a roundtable discussion.

Here, each of us shared our stories. We discussed how we had set up our businesses, the stage we were currently at and what our future plans were. The level of ambition in the room was inspiring.

After each had shared their story, we were asked how many of us had a parent or family who had also started their own business. Eleven out of the twelve ambassadors raised their hands.

It was clear to see how role models are incredibly important when someone is making the decision to start a business. The role model doesn't have to be a parent, it could be a friend, a mentor, or even someone in the media.

Reflection Time: Who are your role models? Who do you look up to?

Contra Deals and Learning How To Cook

A friend of mine, Rachel, had visited Zambia and whilst there realised she didn't really know how to cook. Inspired, she returned to the UK and completed a cooking course at Le Cordon Bleu. Whilst working at a cooking school in central London she began to dream about creating her own school, Rachel's Kitchen. We were catching up and it dawned on us through our conversations that perhaps I could help coach/mentor her through the business side of what she wanted to do. Instead of her paying me, however, we could do a contra deal and she could teach me how to cook. And so, for a number of months, on a weekday night, we would spend a few hours together whilst I learnt how to make a starter, main course and dessert and she learnt some lessons in business.

One of the challenges Rachel was experiencing was her dislike of selling and how she could become comfortable charging £150 for a lesson with ingredients on top. Together we explored the emotional drivers behind the business, and she came up with the idea of sharing the love of food. Instead of thinking about selling her time for money, which is what she thought people were buying, I asked her to take a step back and consider more widely the impact of the cooking lesson. And not just in that moment but in the future.

As she reflected, Rachel understood that not only was the value in learning a particular recipe, but also in gaining confidence in the kitchen: cutting skills, being able to follow a recipe, being able to cook alone and eat more cheaply and healthier, and also cook for family and friends and host meals. It was a deep and enduring life skill and so much more than simply some time exchanged for money. As she put it, it was "helping people to share the love of food". When you put it like that, the cost of the lesson sounds more than reasonable, and this created a shift in how Rachel approached the conversation, giving people the opportunity to buy and benefit from their investment, versus the original perception of being uncomfortable trying to sell to people.

I'm sharing this here in the context of the book due to the nature of the contra deal. Clearly, asking Rachel to teach me how to cook for free wouldn't have cut it! But the exchange was valued by both sides and we were both able to benefit from each other's gifts and experiences.

Reflection Time: What do you have to offer people and what could you get in exchange that would be beneficial? What you can offer and what you would like provide the context for the opportunity and conversation to enable the exchange.

One Young World

One Young World is an awe-inspiring global organisation that gives opportunities to exceptional young people who want to change and are changing the world. It was founded by Kate Robertson and David Jones who have worked tirelessly to provide a platform to help young people contribute and make a difference. I applied and was selected as a delegate in 2013, which gave me not only the opportunity to travel to the summit in South Africa, but also to apply for a speaking slot on the main stage. I chose to pitch a session on youth unemployment, or "youth employment" as I reframed it, as I wanted to talk about entrepreneurship and the ability we all have to create roles, and not just wait for others to provide jobs for us.

Each of the delegate speakers were assigned a One Young World counsellor who included at the time: Sir Bob Geldoff, Sir Richard Branson, Muhammad Yunus and many world leaders from the areas of business, politics and sport. I was excited to be assigned to Arianna Huffington, founder of *The Huffington Post*.

Part I Getting Going

Arianna Huffington & James at One Young World

Thirty minutes before my main stage appearance, I was given a couple of minutes to speak with Arianna. My main concern was making sure she knew what she was going to say in the introduction, but I needn't have worried; she was all over the information. She told me she loved the name of the company, Student Beans, recalling being a young American student at Cambridge University and eating lots of baked beans. I also shared with her the fact my father was at Cambridge studying at the same time she was. In the introduction I was thrilled that she told people to go and look at the website, clearly stating the website and what it did. I couldn't have asked for a better introduction on such a global stage, and it reminded me that successful people are, more often than not, highly engaged in what they're doing—even if you think it's just a little thing to them.

You can find the introduction and speech here:

https://bit.ly/oywje

This is the speech I gave:

* * *

Hello, my name is James Eder and I'm an entrepreneur.

Over the next few minutes I'm going to share with you a story as to how I took control of my future and how you can do the same. How the youth of today can be part of the solution not the problem for youth unemployment. I'm not saying it's easy but it is possible.

In 2002, whilst studying business at the University of Birmingham, I became involved with a charitable/volunteer organisation called AIESEC. When graduating I wanted to give back to the organisation that had given me so much so I applied for a team leadership position. When I wasn't selected I was devastated.

I felt I had failed.

Earlier in my AIESEC experience, a friend bought me a copy of a book called The Naked Leader *with the simple yet powerful questions:*

Imagine if you simply could not fail. Who would you be? Where would you go? What would you do?

In that moment of "failure" I began to question what I really wanted to do. I wanted to give something back and provide opportunities for other people—I realised there were other ways I could do that. Imagine if I could not fail... Despite being just twenty-two, I was inspired to take action.

With an idea I had already created, and a business plan in hand, my brother Michael and I agreed to go into business together. We set up studentbeans.com. The site aims to help students save money and brands to promote themselves to the massive student market.

In the beginning it was tough. We were working eighteen-hour days... We sometimes felt we were not going to make it...

One of the first major hurdles was financing. We got rejected by the bank for a loan. It was then The Prince's Trust who provided $4,500. Not a lot of money, but enough. Critically they also gave us a mentor from a top law firm who was invaluable.

Every day brought new challenges. We had key milestones to reach along the way—achieving breakeven, bringing website development in house, hiring our first employee.

Early on we realised that although we had to have a business plan with milestones, plans do change and that was OK.

Despite the challenges, we kept going and eight years on we're called The Beans Group, we have signed up over 1.2 million users; we have a team of almost forty people working for us and over twenty new job opportunities. We work with brands including Google, Telefonica, Santander and many more. Our mission is to make life a little more awesome and our twenty-five-year vision is to touch the lives of over 100 million young people every day.

My biggest challenge when I left university was finding a job. My biggest challenge now is finding the best talent to take the business forward. You can do the same.

It isn't just about setting up a business as it's unlikely we'll all do that. However, it is about being proactive and about taking responsibility for your contribution in the world.

With this in mind there are many things I have learnt along the way but there are three key things I would like to leave you with.

Firstly, take action. Ideas are cheap but it's those that take action who can really make a difference in the world. One Young World 2013, I stand here today. I shared my vision today and my commitment to you. I ask you now all to stand up with me as a sign that you too believe you can be the force to change and as a commitment you are part of the solution. Please stand up.

As we stand together, my second point is learn by doing. There is only so much you can learn by studying and preparing but the real learning takes place when you are taking action.

Thirdly, keep going. If it was easy, everyone would be doing it.

So, what are you waiting for?

Life isn't a rehearsal. The time is now and it's up to us all. Thank you.

* * *

The response from the speech was overwhelming. I remember that, in advance, the organisers were unsure about engaging the audience to stand. But having convinced them it would be a really rousing moment, they positioned me as the final speech of six in the youth unemployment section.

Following the event I spoke to many people who commented on that moment. Finding a way to put yourself in front of people can be an incredible boost to your profile and gives people a reason to talk to you. And once you're talking, the conversation can go anywhere.

As well as the opportunity to speak on stage, I was given the chance to have lunch with a group called "the B-Team". This is a group of leaders who believe that, together, they can create a new system that will benefit both people and the planet. Members include Sir Richard Branson, Arianna Huffington and Paul Polman, at the time CEO of Unilever. Unfortunately, having applied to join that session, I was unsuccessful.

And so, at another plenary session instead, I found myself having to step out to go to the toilet. I don't like to do that, but when you gotta go, you gotta go! In the corridor I passed Ella, one of the organisers, now the Managing Director, who recognised me from my session and seemed to know I'd been unsuccessful in my application for the lunch. She stopped me and told me there was actually some additional space at the last minute if I would like to join.

The timing was incredible. Of course I said yes, and even had a short chat reconnecting with Arianna Huffington on the way over.

When we entered the room I had to make a choice of where to sit and, recognising that many of the B-Team weren't there yet, I decided to sit on the table with the most vacant seats. As the room filled up I found myself seated with some of Sir Richard Branson's extended entourage, and a number of local business leaders who didn't really seem to understand why they were there.

I felt like I'd made a strategic call but it hadn't panned out. I was in the right room, but at the wrong table.

As it happened, one of the full-time employees of the B-Team was an old friend from AIESEC, Raj, who'd gone to Strathclyde University and I'd originally met him in Sweden in 2003. He recognised me as the food arrived and came to say hello. But before he left he spoke to the person next to me and they quietly left. I thought nothing more of it until, a few moments later, Nobel Peace Prize winner and founder of Grameen Bank (a micro-lending platform that strives to help people out of poverty) Muhammad Yunus was placed next to me.

It was a fortunate turn of events, and I'm not really sure why it happened, but I'm glad it did. We chatted for some time about a host of things, but the most impactful moment for me came when I asked him why he chose to do what he does.

"Trust," he said. "Trust you are doing the right thing, you are where you are meant to be, doing what you are meant to be doing".

When I'm feeling overwhelmed I think back to this and focus on the fact I'm doing what I can do. If someone who could have chosen to do almost anything was content doing his bit, then I can be too. It's something I'd urge everyone to be comfortable with.

One Young World was the most incredible experience giving young people the world stage amongst some of the most incredible inspiring thought leaders of our time. Whether that be Ellen MacArthur talking about the circular economy, Sir Bob Geldof challenging us all to do better and be better and Paul Polman who I mentioned was CEO of Unilever at the time driving the sustainability agenda and instead of making it an add on and something nice to have, very much integrating their sustainability into the brand strategy. Lifebuoy for example runs one of the world's largest hand-washing behaviour change interventions. Lifebuoy has also created alphabet books, board games, teaching aids, and digital games to make hand hygiene an integral part of the school curriculum. This is very much aligned and core to the message of Who Cares Wins: Why Good Business is Better Business by David Jones the co-founder of One Young World.

One of the messages Paul shared in his speech that I am frequently reminded of;

> *If you want to go fast go alone,*
> *if you want to go far go together.*
> African Proverb

This holds true when building anything from a community to a business, a project or anything sustainable if you want to create a legacy and build something that isn't just reliant on you. The Collision Code I hope will help contribute to start these connections that will help you succeed and go that much further.

Reflection Time: In what ways can you apply the lessons of taking action, learning through experience and trusting your journey to your own aspirations, and how will you embrace the opportunities that come your way to make a positive impact?

Building Your Profile

There's a lot to be said for building your profile. I've seen the correlation. Ultimately the more known you are the more opportunities present themselves and find you. This has been demonstrated almost without fail, every time I've spoken on a stage or on a podcast or interview or been featured in the marketing press or newspapers, or winning awards. These all contribute to building your profile for others to see.

One of the habits from Stephen Covey's *The 7 Habits of Highly Effective People* is start with the end in mind. What is it that you want to achieve? What do you want to be known for? Then do everything that aligns and work backwards from that.

Raising your profile makes it easy for others to connect with you as it gives them more context to reach out and be in touch. They know what you're interested in and what you're passionate about, what you're looking for and how you can help them.

Someone who has always inspired me in this space is Daniel Priestley, entrepreneur and founder of Dent. He's written a number of best-selling books including *The Key Person of Influence*. I met Daniel when he just arrived in the UK and we've met many times over the years. He was part of the ICE community I mention in the resources section towards the end of the book, one of the entrepreneurial networks I've been part of. It's inspiring to see what he's built over the years, the content he shares and how he shows up so consistently.

Reflection Time: If you were to be known for something, what would you want to be known for? If you were to be interviewed, what publication would you want to be featured in? If you were to put content out or write a book, what would it be about?

Always Ask

This isn't the first book I've had published. For the first six years of Student Beans I even wrote a daily journal with a view to telling that story. I even gave it a title, "Behind the Beans". However, as I approached my thirtieth birthday, I attended the book launch of *SuperBusiness: How I Started SuperJam from My Gran's Kitchen* written by a friend and fellow entrepreneur Fraser Doherty, founder of SuperJam. (Incidentally we'd met whilst both speaking at a conference in Warwick and I ended up giving him a lift back to London.) At the event I shared my dream of publishing a book, and Fraser offered to introduce me to his literary agent, Jonathan Conway.

After the event I followed up with Fraser in an email and, a few days later, an email came in from his agent with an offer to meet. As it happens, the agent had gone to the same school as me and was even in the same year as my brother.

I shared my dream about writing "Behind the Beans", but because the story was still (and still is) unfolding, he asked if instead I'd consider publishing a student cookbook. At the time my cooking skills were pretty non-existent, but I could see the appeal.

We found a fantastic home economist and recipe writer Rob Allison who was able to write, curate and test all of the recipes for us and we gave all the recipes a "student" twist, such as using a pint glass for measuring ingredients.

The book was pitched to various publishers and Amanda Harris at Orion at the time ended up beating the competition by offering a two-book deal that resulted in both *The Ultimate Student Cookbook* and *The Healthy Student Cookbook*. Both books got great coverage, and John Torode from BBC TV's *Masterchef* bought a copy for his son, which was a nice moment. We also had a ten-page colour supplement included in *The Times* as part of a "back to university" campaign (the sort of thing that really convinces friends and family you're doing something "proper").

It's a good reminder that if you want help in making something happen, ask someone who's done it before. More often than not people want to help out, and to see others succeed as well. What you often find is there are people in your network who've gone through the challenges you're facing, and with a little digging you can find those worth reaching out to for advice.

Reflection Time: Who in your network could you reach out to for support or advice on your goals, and what's one simple step you can take today to connect with them?

YMS: Youth Marketing Strategy

As I was nearing graduation, with the experience of being a brand manager at Yell.com, Simon, my eldest brother, was working at Haymarket, the publishers for their conferences and events division. One of the divisions was putting on a Marketing to Students conference and was conveniently looking for people for their student brand manager panel. Simon put me forward and I was invited to take part. It was an interesting day as I was on the cusp of graduation. Student Beans was little more than an idea and business plan at this stage and, more than that, at the time I didn't know that we were going to acquire a business and launch our own Marketing to Students conference.

Over the following years we sponsored and collaborated with the Marketing to Students conference in various ways including chairing the conference one year.

Reach Students, run by Luke Mitchell, produced research in the space which we followed. It was then in 2011 he created Youth Marketing Strategy, a conference for brands, agencies and media owners interested in those aged sixteen to twenty-four. We sponsored it. The stars aligned as Simon then joined the business in 2012. There was an opportunity to acquire Reach Students and bring it into the mix at The Beans Group, and grow Youth Marketing Strategy under a new brand at the time called Voxburner helping brands understand the youth market through research, insights and events. In 2012 we launched the first Youth Marketing Strategy, YMS, run by us with 120 people at the IMAX cinema in London Waterloo. YMS has since grown to become the world's largest youth marketing conference, taking place in the UK and the US every year, with over 2,000 attendees.

Richard Jackson, who took on the running of YMS, summed it up for me after receiving feedback from clients that national and global brands are basing their strategies and marketing decisions based on attending our events. It's just an amazing testament to what the team has built over the years. Conferences are a microcosm of what *The Collision Code* aims to achieve: they provide permission, context and a supportive environment that fosters the confidence needed to connect with others. It's an event that people look forward to and one of the main events each year where the industry really unites.

YMS is not just for the well-known brands but ultimately a platform for up and coming businesses over the years to launch and grow, including the well-known speaker, investor, entrepreneur and now BBC Dragon, Steven Bartlett. Steven was first involved with YMS in 2015, thanks to his newly formed business, Social Chain. Speaking then about "The Kids Who Decide What All The Other Kids Talk About", he and other members of the Social Chain team have joined us on the YMS stages at London, New York or San Francisco nearly every year since.

In January 2024 the Voxburner brand was retired and YMS and Student Beans now sit under the parent brand Pion! Pion helps brands with verification, advertising and insights, positioning the company for continued success and growth for the years ahead as they approach their twentieth anniversary since founding in June 2005.

The Marketing Academy

In November 2011 I was in London attending an event with thirty American VCs and entrepreneurs. One of the organisers of the group included Sherry Coutu CBE and Reid Hoffman, founder of LinkedIn, all in town as part of "Silicon Valley Comes to the UK", a programme seeking to transfer knowledge from the US market to businesses operating out of the UK. It was an amazing opportunity to be in the room and connect with the community.

During the event we were split into different rooms for panel sessions and I was placed with other companies who were unfunded. Shortly after starting, however, an alarm went off (as it happens, a bomb scare), and we were all forced to evacuate. Standing around outside I got chatting to Gregor, the founder of Morphsuits (all-in-one costumes that cover body, limbs and head!). As we chatted, it turned out he also knew Emanuel, who I'd met on my AIESEC adventures. And he agreed with Emanuel that I would get lots out of this mysterious thing called "The Marketing Academy".

The Marketing Academy is an incredible programme for which the business world, and world in general, should be thankful. It offers scholarships for the best emerging (and established) leadership talent in marketing, media and advertising by providing a nine-month programme of development that is quite unreal. Gregor told me when nominations were likely to open, and I made a note to keep an eye out.

When the time came, I was one of around 500 people nominated for The Marketing Academy (you need a third party to put your name forward, and I asked Emanuel). After the initial application process and showcase I was thrilled to make it down to the final sixty where I'd face an interview from Bupa's HR director at the time Craig McCoy and James Hart a senior VP of AVG, the antivirus software company.

But before that was booked in, I had been invited to speak at an event at Hertfordshire University.

As often happens at these events you get chatting to the other speakers, and I found myself deep in conversation with Zak Sos from Reuters. As he was heading back to a similar area of London, I offered him a lift as I'd driven. He was planning to get the train back so declined, but as I went to leave he was some way back in the taxi queue and this time accepted my offer. On the way home we chatted about what we were up to over the coming days.

The next day I got a call from Zak (we'd swapped numbers, always swap numbers) thanking me for the lift and telling me that they'd discussed The Marketing Academy in the office that morning, and would I be open to Reuters following my interview process to broadcast on TV.

I was excited about the filming, but, of course, I didn't want to jeopardise the wider opportunity The Marketing Academy was offering. The added pressure of being recorded worried me a little, but I thought it would be great publicity for everyone. The Marketing Academy were brilliant and said it was up to me if I wanted to be filmed before and after, but they said the actual interview process could not be on camera, which was fair. So phone calls were made, all the parties agreed to be involved and I ended up becoming a feature on Reuters, along with a live recording when I found out whether I'd been accepted or not (spoiler, I was—thankfully!).

You can watch the video here: https://bit.ly/jereuters

At the start of The Marketing Academy I felt like an entrepreneur on an island. By the end of the core programme, I felt like a totally embedded part of the marketing community with opportunity after opportunity presenting itself from a whole range of brilliant people. I benefited from countless hours of mentoring, training and development and was able to take advantage of last-minute offers to meet the likes of Carolyn McCall, CEO of easyJet and Jon Goldstone, head of food and ice cream at Unilever, when others with less flexible schedules had to drop out.

In summary, The Marketing Academy (https://themarketingacademy.org/uk/) provides scholarships for those in marketing and entrepreneurs in the UK, USA and Australia. Through a combination of training, development, mentoring and coaching this immersive programme takes rocks and turns them into diamonds. As part of the programme all participants also experience The Living Leader programme, (https://www.thelivingleader.com). I was fortunate enough to be trained by the founder, Penny Ferguson, who challenged and inspired us, breaking us down to build us back up. A special mention and credit also goes to Sherilyn Shackell, the founder of The Marketing Academy, who has worked tirelessly for the marketing community providing something for the community that transcends generations and is helping shape the leadership in some of the largest brands in the world to some of the newest start-ups aspiring to make their mark.

At one mentoring session with Russ Lidstone, at the time CEO of global media agency Havas London, we covered a lot of ground and, towards the end, he offered to introduce me to Kate Robertson, who at the time was UK group chair of Havas, who had also co-founded One Young World alongside David Jones. The introduction followed, but we never found a time to meet and, as these things sometimes do, it petered out.

But then something serendipitous happened. Another scholar on The Marketing Academy had been nominated for the Women in Marketing awards and asked me to tag along with her. It was there that I actually bumped into Kate (who was there to receive a lifetime achievement award) and I used the opportunity to speak to her face to face. With the connection to Russ, she was happy to organise something and introduced me to her assistant to sort something out.

When I visited her at her office she listened intently to my journey and told me about One Young World. She suggested I apply as a delegate for the next summit in South Africa (you already read how that turned out, and can hopefully see how opportunities interlink with other opportunities and become far more than the sum of their parts).

But it's funny how these stepping stones appear. Emanuel knew Gregor, who both knew The Marketing Academy and thought I'd be a good fit. Then Zak and Reuters made me think there really was something in this, and the rest snowballed from there.

* * *

The Marketing Academy really did keep on giving. At one point an email arrived from the office saying that a member of the team at Sainsbury's had offered some tickets for the filming of *What's Cooking from the Sainsbury's Kitchen* presented by Lisa Faulkner and Ben Shepherd. I immediately responded and secured a ticket. The studio had been created in a Sainsbury's car park and it was a really fun day seeing how the programme came together.

After the event I reached out to the organiser Sarah Ellis and mentioned the upcoming launch of *The Ultimate Student Cookbook* and wondered if they had any interest in stocking the book. It turns out they did, and they were actively looking for books, and other items, targeting students in some of their most relevant stores. It became one of the biggest orders for the books and was a really nice example of dots being joined thanks to grasping a seemingly random opportunity.

* * *

On another occasion I ended my day at a networking event in central London and, as I sometimes do, asked the host if there was anyone in the room they thought I should meet.

The Collision Code

It's not something I do often, but it can be a great way to get the conversation started especially when there's a lot of people in the room. As it happened the person I was introduced to was Laura Hagan who worked for Dyson. This shouldn't seem that remarkable, but it was.

"Dyson?" I said, astonished, "I've just won a Dyson DC30 handheld cleaner. It's in the cloakroom now!"

To rewind several hours, I'd started the day at PHD, the communications agency, on a full immersive session organised by The Marketing Academy where we were tasked with coming up with ideas for one of their clients, Dyson. This itself was bizarre, as just that morning our vacuum cleaner in the flat had broken (not a Dyson!) after not much use. I'd originally bought it because it was cheaper; a false economy it turned out.

At the PHD session, I told this story, alongside my memory of using a Dyson hand dryer for the first time. It was in a restaurant, and I remember returning to the table astonished at how wonderful it was. It's not often you're moved by any brand, let alone a hand dryer.

In the end we developed an idea around education, partnering with schools to run projects related to the actual mechanics of Dyson's products, supported by experiential installations in shopping centres and the like to really bring the technology to life. The idea of inviting people to literally get inside a giant Dyson and take part in indoor skydiving certainly seemed exciting to me, and it clearly captured the panel's imagination when we presented because we won. The prize? A Dyson for everyone in the team.

After the networking event, I followed up with Laura and I ended up being invited to Dyson's HQ in Wiltshire to share my ideas and experiences with their Group Marketing Director, Adam Rostom. It was in this meeting that I also met Tammy Potter who introduced me to Wavelength which formed part of my next leadership and development journey. I was also given a discount to the web store which I could use to replace my broken vacuum cleaner! It's amazing how these journeys unravel, and how your enthusiasm alone can put you somewhere you didn't ever expect to be.

* * *

When I first found out about The Marketing Academy and was nominated back in early 2012, I knew it was something special. I remember speaking to our board and sharing with them that this opportunity was like no other and asking them to endorse my application. On reflection this couldn't have been more true. Over my years as a scholar and beyond, I've been exposed to hundreds of hours of contact time—from sessions with mentors, faculty days and boot camps, to lunches, dinners and drinks. Reflecting on this experience, I thought I should share a selection of key inspirational people and learnings that have helped me on my journey with The Marketing Academy.

1. Russ Lidstone, at the time CEO at Havas Worldwide London. I got an overwhelming sense that he runs an organisation that lives and breathes doing good. By doing good, this can also be beneficial for business and the two aren't mutually exclusive.

2. Carolyn McCall, at the time CEO of EasyJet. Seeing first hand her passion and high energy. Her commitment to getting things done, being approachable and at the same time tough and firm when needed.

3. Simon Biltcliffe, at the time, CEO of Webmart. He ran a session at boot camp and welcomed us into his office instilling ideals that included: 1) you have to share, 2) no such thing as a competitor, and 3) look after others and they will look after you.

4. Ita Murphy, at the time Managing Director of Mindshare. A formidable person to meet. She said three things that stuck with me: network now for the job you want in five years' time, to get clients to love you think from their perspective, and have a cup of tea and listen to people—it is often through listening that the real difference can be made.

5. Amanda Mackenzie OBE, at the time CMO for Aviva PLC. She spoke passionately about believing in something, driving it forward and making it happen, but also shared some practical tips about networking. She said think of networking instead as "net giving"—how you can help other people and add value that can make a real difference to them. If at an event you meet just one person, have an authentic interesting conversation and are able to help them, that is likely to be more than what most people in the room have done. It's this net giving concept that I approach everyday collisions with. Being open to how you can help instead of what you can get I believe opens you up to so many more connections and opportunities.

6. Shaa Wasmund MBE, *Sunday Times* best-selling author and entrepreneur. She ran a session at the third and final boot camp raising the energy in the room with her "stop talking, start doing" attitude helping people to confront what they really wanted, what was stopping them or holding them back and then coached them through how they can make their wants a reality. Powerful and direct—listening to Shaa makes you think anything is possible.

7. Oli Barrett, connector, presenter and co-creator. He is someone who truly lives and breathes *The Collision Code*. Whenever I mention this book or its concepts, people immediately ask, "Have you met Oli?"

Our paths have crossed countless times over the years—whether when he co-founded Startup Britain, hosting and compering at more events than I can count, or even skiing together. Often described as one of the most connected people in the world, Oli has an incredible ability to bring people together in ways that lead to real impact. The session he ran at The Marketing Academy boot camp was no exception.

What sets Oli apart isn't just the breadth of his network, but the generosity and intention with which he connects people. He doesn't just introduce for the sake of it—he actively listens, understands what people need, and finds the right person who can help. One of his signature questions is: "If there were one person I could introduce you to that would make a real difference, who would it be?"

More often than not, if that person is in the room, Oli will make the introduction on the spot. If not, you can be sure he'll follow up and make it happen later. His ability to connect people at exactly the right time is what makes him such a powerful force in the world of networking, entrepreneurship and beyond.

Oli isn't just a connector—he's a catalyst. The introductions he makes don't just spark conversations; they ignite opportunities, partnerships and lifelong collaborations.

There are so many more examples and learnings. Above all be bold, take action and be responsible for your leadership journey and the impact you have.

Reflection Time: Looking back on your own experiences, what's one unexpected connection or opportunity that has shaped your journey, and how can you remain open to discovering more like it in the future?

The DO Lectures and Getting Things Done

In 2013 I attended an event by The DO Lectures (https://thedolectures.com/) hosted by David Hieatt and his team in Cardigan in Wales. The theme of the event was DO Start-up, all about making ideas come to life.

It was an amazing, immersive few days with around 100 attendees, sleeping in yurts, showering outside, eating amazing food and spending evenings around a campfire. It was really magical. It was also very special that most, if not all, of the speakers were also attendees at the event so there was no green room. There was a real opportunity to get to know people and connect.

On the last day they held an auction to raise money for the local community. Many local people had lost their jobs due to manufacturing going abroad so needed support for retraining and to stop a negative trend of unemployment and the associated challenges.

One of the opportunities available in the auction was to have time with the author and founder of the "Getting Things Done" methodology, David Allen. I remember, before the bidding started, standing up and endorsing his work and how amazing it was. A few years earlier I had the pleasure of doing some training with Ed Lamont who works closely with David and delivers the training in the UK. It was amazing training that transformed the way I worked with a lasting impact even to today with multiple techniques even helping me write this book. The public course at the time was around £500 per day so the opportunity to work one-to-one with David directly would be such a gift. As the bidding started I was underwhelmed with how little interest there was so I decided to bid on behalf of Student Beans with a view to getting him to run a session for the team. To my delight and surprise I won the bid for not much more than the cost of two places on their public training course.

The day we spoke, David was just about to deliver the closing speech at the Evernote conference in San Francisco. To say I was excited was an understatement. As we spoke, I explained what we were doing as a business and I asked if it was possible the next time he was in the UK if I could use the prize for him to run a session for Student Beans at our offices in Kentish Town. We were about forty people at the time.

Around six months later David and his wife Kathryn came to our offices. The day was transformative and an overwhelming success. It was game changing in helping people in the team be more effective and "get things done".

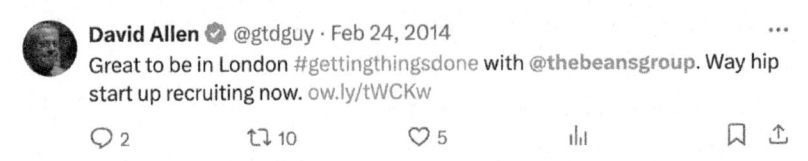

> **David Allen** ✓ @gtdguy · Feb 24, 2014
> Great to be in London #gettingthingsdone with @thebeansgroup. Way hip start up recruiting now. ow.ly/tWCKw
>
> 💬 2   🔁 10   ♡ 5

If you've not heard of "Getting Things Done" before I'd really recommend it. It's one of those things that you hear about and wonder why they don't teach this stuff in schools. Absolutely game changing.

Reflection Time: It doesn't always need to be the case, but what ways can you align your charitable giving with your personal or professional objectives that could make a real difference for you, your community and those that you are donating to?

Part II

Making Connections

Let's Talk

For years, when I'd talk about the ideas outlined in this book, I'd start with this story.

I was sitting on the London Underground when someone sat in the empty seat next to me. They were clutching a CV/resume, which caught my eye because I was deep in a recruitment round for Student Beans. So I thought I'd use this common ground to start a conversation.

"Are you interviewing for jobs? What sort of thing are you looking for?"

His name was Nick Johnston and yes, he was job hunting. I told him I was the founder of a company and we were looking for all sorts of people. If he had a copy of his CV I'd happily take it and let him know if we had anything that suited. Back at the office I ran the CV by Michael and we agreed there were a couple of roles he would be well suited to. So we invited him in.

During the initial interview Michael asked Nick how he'd met me. From his perspective, he was just sitting quietly minding his own business when I did the very un-London thing of making conversation. What we didn't know was Nick's girlfriend worked for Orion, publishers of the Student Beans cookbooks, and even though it was yet to be released at that point, she knew all about us and reassured him I wasn't completely mad!

Nick ended up coming to work for us supporting Michael in a number of ways, including recruitment (though we never found anyone else on the Underground). It's a great tale of serendipity, and taking a chance—for me, and for Nick.

Sometimes the pieces of the puzzle are out there, just waiting to be connected.

In October 2010 I was at the office talking to William Harris, one of our business development team. We were discussing Virgin Experience Days, which were run by a company called Acorne, and trying to work out how Student Beans could work with them directly. Meeting concluded, I headed to Golders Green station to head into town. As I got there an announcement was made over the loudspeaker. It sounded important, but I couldn't hear it, so I turned to the person next to me.

"Is there a problem with the trains?"

I was told it was fine and the train would be coming soon.

I continued the conversation (but of course I did!)

"You're all dressed up, where are you off to?" The man was in full black tie.

He told me he was on his way to an awards ceremony for "points and loyalty".

"That's interesting," I said, and asked what he did.

"Oh, you won't have heard of us, but do you know Virgin Experience Days? Well, I work for Acorne. We're the company that actually powers the experiences."

I mean, you couldn't make this up if you tried. It turned out he was a business development manager, literally the person we needed to speak to in order to build a partnership. We continued all the way into Holborn together, and when I got off I immediately called William. His name was Darren Ziff and I followed up afterwards leading to a partnership.

By this point in my life I was spotting these connections more and more. By having conversations, things would happen. And I started to think whether there was a way to maximise the potential that was clearly here, there and all around us.

With this in mind, I started to look for inspiration everywhere.

At an event I spoke at called Tutor2u, students were pitching ideas. One of them was a bracelet you could wear to remind you to eat your five-a-day fruits and vegetables. A while later I saw Sam Conniff, founder of Livity and author of *Be More Pirate*, speaking at an event. He was wearing a badge with a simple call to action to "be more pirate". The two stuck in my head. Was there something I could do that would trigger a similar response to get people to talk to each other?

At yet another event, I met Angus George, a creative director at Ogilvy and another member of The Marketing Academy community. He was wearing a badge that read "Hangover on board", a pastiche of Transport for London's "Baby on board" badges used by pregnant women to indicate they may be in need of a seat. I was sold on badges. But I wasn't quite sure how…

During the Olympics of 2012, London exploded with friendliness. One common theme I spotted was the power of uniforms worn by the "games makers", volunteers who would direct people between venues and answer questions from visitors. Just having that T-shirt on made it easy to talk to them. It gave added permission within an already fertile context.

We started out talking about meeting Nick on the tube. The CV in his hand was the context that provided me with permission to engage him. As you've heard, by now, I had done this so many times that confidence was no longer an issue for me! And I kept thinking, *How can we, as a society, have more of those moments?* Not CVs, of course, but something.

Badges. Badges that break the ice and allow you permission to say hello. And just like that, FriendlyFriday was born. A movement to get the world talking, one hello at a time. A way to capture potential opportunities.

I loved the idea. I knew there was something in it. But... where next?

* * *

I've already told you about my experiences at One Young World in 2013. At the end of the summit everyone was given a ribbon and asked to write on it an action they would take as a result of the experience. I wrote "Launch FriendlyFriday", the name I had by now given to this idea I had for bringing the world together and to talk to each other more often. At the end of the closing ceremony of One Young World all the ribbons are wrapped into one big ball that takes centre stage. It's a really powerful moment. I knew I now had to do my bit and make it happen.

The idea for FriendlyFriday was simple: wear a badge to say you're open to being spoken to and that badge gives people explicit permission to engage with you. In developing the idea, I was thinking of shared passions for a football team, or people who have dogs or babies with them, or even people who wave at each other on the road because they're driving the same car (Minis, Beetles, MX5s, etc.). All simple reasons to say hello. Why the name FriendlyFriday? Well,

Fridays seem to be a more friendly day and if you think it's Friday, it's the end of the week and people have more of a spring to their step and seem happier.

I also wanted to make the badges "viral", by encouraging people to give badges to others around them. They would be distributed in packs of two, and by wearing a badge they would make themselves open to conversation. Eventually they'd be everywhere (and then, maybe, wouldn't be needed anymore!).

I was finally pushed to take action to make this a reality when Olivia, a member of the Student Beans team, showed me a pack of four badges she'd spotted with positive slogans on them reading "fun", "happy", "love" and "play". The pack was so nice, but so simple, and it didn't feel overwhelming to get something like that produced.

As a side story Olivia and I went to University together and studied the same course. In 2010 I had a meeting with You-Gov to explore some ideas of how we could collaborate and it just so happens Olivia was in the meeting. A few months later we bumped into each other again at Marketing Week Live and industry conference whilst waiting for the train home we spoke and shortly after she reached out asking about job opportunities. She's now been in the business over 14 years and we worked closely together in her role as PR and Marketing and then organising the world's largest Marketing to Student Conferences YMS. I'm so grateful to everything she has done and does - any project we worked together on, things just got done, she anticipated what I needed and made things happen. Thank you Olivia.

The same day Olivia showed me the pack of badges, I reached out to Simon Kay, an old school friend who ran a promotional merchandise company. He'd previously contacted me about doing some work for Student Beans, and while we didn't need anything, I sounded him out about doing a test run of the badges for free. He loved the idea and agreed, so now we were actually up and running.

The final packs were designed thanks to another favour from a friend from The Marketing Academy who liked the idea, Robbie Dale (who has since played a significant part in getting this book in your hands too) and featured two badges that read "Say hello" and had the FriendlyFriday website on them. One was to keep, one to share. In each pack were also instructions on how to use them with sample opening lines to provide a bit more support and confidence.

To create a sense of occasion for launching the idea, I organised some workshops at companies and schools and events where people could hear a bit of the story behind FriendlyFriday and, of course, get some badges into the hands of the public. People either donated £2 towards the FriendlyFriday Foundation or the businesses/events paid for them. I ran a number of events at Wayra, Pitch at the Palace and media agency StackWorks over the course of a few months.

The Collision Code

The FriendlyFriday Foundation was an additional idea I had to make a positive impact with the project by providing support and investment for young people around the UK looking to start a nonprofit or social enterprise. It was all starting to feel very exciting. Now this existed, it was brilliant to explore what I could do with it.

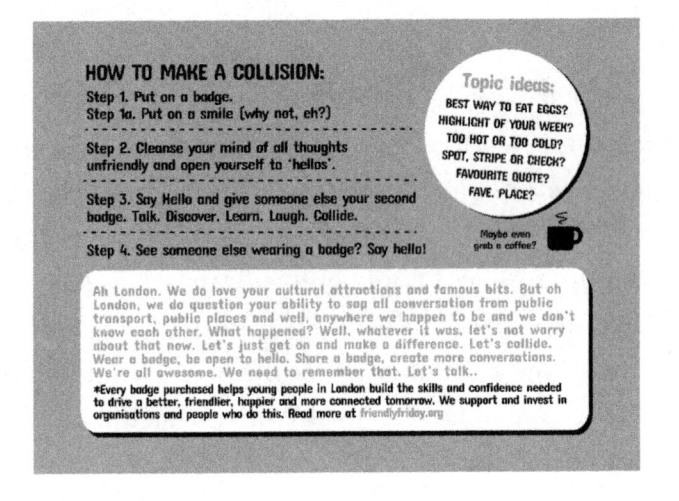

ARE YOU READY TO COLLIDE?

Say Hello
friendlyfriday.org

Say Hello
friendlyfriday.org

*Minimum Donation £2

HAD A COLLISION? LET US KNOW:
Share it on Twitter @friendlyfriday #collision

(It makes us smile & generates 1 fluid oz of additional goodwill in the world)

HOW TO MAKE A COLLISION:
Step 1. Put on a badge.
Step 1a. Put on a smile (why not, eh?)

Step 2. Cleanse your mind of all thoughts unfriendly and open yourself to 'hellos'.

Step 3. Say Hello and give someone else your second badge. Talk. Discover. Learn. Laugh. Collide.

Step 4. See someone else wearing a badge? Say hello!

Topic ideas:
BEST WAY TO EAT EGGS?
HIGHLIGHT OF YOUR WEEK?
TOO HOT OR TOO COLD?
SPOT, STRIPE OR CHECK?
FAVOURITE QUOTE?
FAVE. PLACE?

Maybe even grab a coffee?

Ah London. We do love your cultural attractions and famous bits. But oh London, we do question your ability to sap all conversation from public transport, public places and well, anywhere we happen to be and we don't know each other. What happened? Well, whatever it was, let's not worry about that now. Let's just get on and make a difference. Let's collide. Wear a badge, be open to hello. Share a badge, create more conversations. We're all awesome. We need to remember that. Let's talk..

*Every badge purchased helps young people in London build the skills and confidence needed to drive a better, friendlier, happier and more connected tomorrow. We support and invest in organisations and people who do this. Read more at friendlyfriday.org

Part II Making Connections

I was approached by Telefonica to run a session at One Young World in Dublin in 2014, focused on networking. Naturally, it was a great opportunity to marry these worlds. I even invested in creating some bespoke One Young World badges for the event.

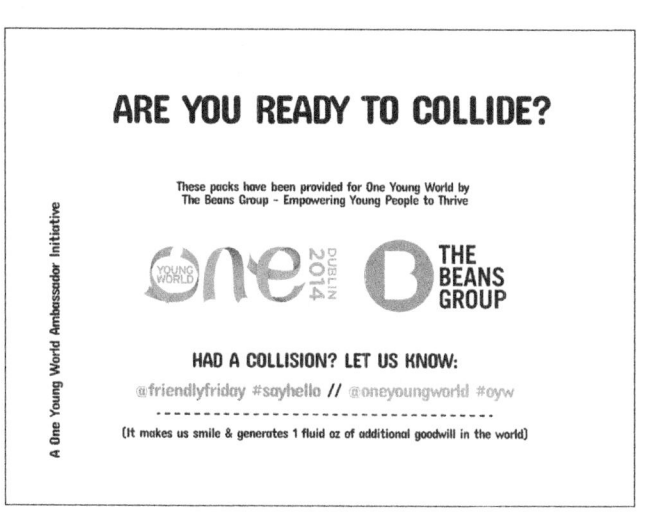

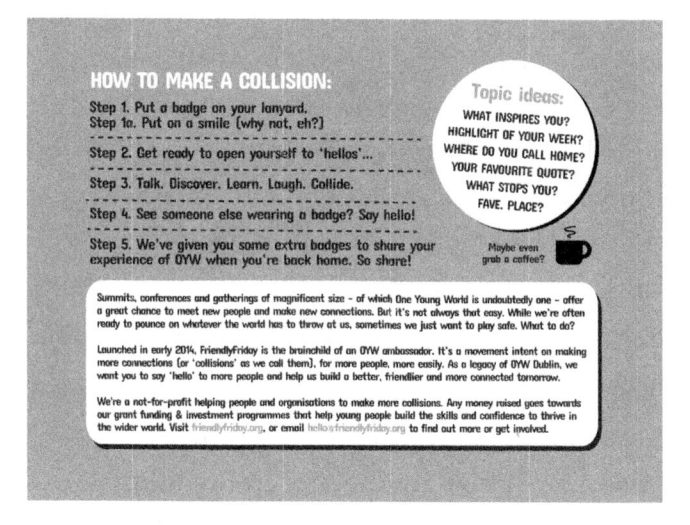

ARE YOU READY TO COLLIDE?

These packs have been provided for One Young World by
The Beans Group – Empowering Young People to Thrive

one YOUNG WORLD DUBLIN 2014   THE BEANS GROUP

HAD A COLLISION? LET US KNOW:

@friendlyfriday #sayhello // @oneyoungworld #oyw

(It makes us smile & generates 1 fluid oz of additional goodwill in the world)

A One Young World Ambassador Initiative

HOW TO MAKE A COLLISION:

Step 1. Put a badge on your lanyard.
Step 1a. Put on a smile (why not, eh?)
Step 2. Get ready to open yourself to 'hellos'...
Step 3. Talk. Discover. Learn. Laugh. Collide.
Step 4. See someone else wearing a badge? Say hello!
Step 5. We've given you some extra badges to share your experience of OYW when you're back home. So share!

Topic ideas:
WHAT INSPIRES YOU?
HIGHLIGHT OF YOUR WEEK?
WHERE DO YOU CALL HOME?
YOUR FAVOURITE QUOTE?
WHAT STOPS YOU?
FAVE. PLACE?

Maybe even grab a coffee?

Summits, conferences and gatherings of magnificent size – of which One Young World is undoubtedly one – offer a great chance to meet new people and make new connections. But it's not always that easy. While we're often ready to pounce on whatever the world has to throw at us, sometimes we just want to play safe. What to do?

Launched in early 2014, FriendlyFriday is the brainchild of an OYW ambassador. It's a movement intent on making more connections (or 'collisions' as we call them), for more people, more easily. As a legacy of OYW Dublin, we want you to say 'hello' to more people and help us build a better, friendlier and more connected tomorrow.

We're a not-for-profit helping people and organisations to make more collisions. Any money raised goes towards our grant funding & investment programmes that help young people build the skills and confidence to thrive in the wider world. Visit friendlyfriday.org, or email hello@friendlyfriday.org to find out more or get involved.

The Collision Code

I already had an engagement in Frankfurt speaking at UNESCO about entrepreneurship and youth unemployment, which meant flying straight from Germany to Dublin. My plan was therefore to finalise my presentation on the flight. On boarding, I tried to start a conversation, as I do, with the passenger next to me, but she swiftly closed me down and clearly didn't want to engage. So I turned to the man on the other side of me and started a conversation. It turned out he was going to One Young World too. As we chatted, I walked him through my slides and gave him a load of badges for him and his colleagues at Siemens.

I was hoping to get the badges into the delegate packs for the event, but logistics hadn't allowed for it. Instead I ran a couple of pre-conference networking events, alongside the Telefonica session.

The next few days were filled with speaking, connecting and sharing packs of badges with anyone and everyone. By the end of the conference it was thrilling to see them pinned to lanyards everywhere you looked, and so satisfying to see the real-world application of an idea that had been a mere flicker of an idea just a year earlier. The feedback was positive, people told me they loved the story behind it and I think it inspired a lot of extra conversation.

FriendlyFriday badges existed to give people a new context to connect. I believe most people want that, most of the time. Even the woman on the plane who didn't want to chat

Part II *Making Connections*

to a stranger, but seemed interested after the fact, may not really have wanted to be left alone, but lacked the confidence and structure to dive into that conversation. Which isn't a criticism, if anything it's the norm. It's hard and scary to be vulnerable and open yourself to someone totally new. But, as I hope this book is showing, when you do, the upsides can be huge.

Of course, people don't generally have a badge doing the heavy lifting. So it's up to you to find a suitable context that gives you the confidence to connect. As long as you do, you have permission to say hello, or ask someone a question. You can't expect everyone to be enthusiastic, or even to give you an answer, but as long as you're respectful and polite, then it's the human thing to engage with those around you. If you need more permission than that, then I'll give it to you now. You have permission to connect with other people as long as the context allows. There you go!

* * *

Whenever you launch a new project, or get obsessed with an idea, you start to spot similar things everywhere. In this case, badges. One morning I heard about a man who'd produced some "Tube Chat" badges to encourage people to talk on the tube, but had received lots of negative feedback and press.

Given my interest in the area, I thought I'd phone up the *Evening Standard* who had covered the negativity the badges had inspired. I was thinking I could reference World Say Hello Day and explain why I thought these badges didn't work, but why FriendlyFriday could.

"Hello, *Evening Standard* news desk…"

I launched into my pitch. The woman at the other end was curt. No, she told me. The badges don't work because nobody wants to talk to each other. By the pace and tone of her voice I could feel she just wanted me off the phone. I quickly ended the call. Not every interaction goes the way you want it to!

FriendlyFriday became less of a focus at the time, although very much lives through the concepts of this book. You can still visit www.friendlyfriday.org for more information.

No matter your enthusiasm and efforts, sometimes it's just not the right time. I wonder, for example, how it might have worked as we emerged from the COVID-19 pandemic. It's important not to be hard on yourself if an idea doesn't pan out. Specifically, because it's just one execution of that idea. The key is to not lose heart in the insight or epiphany that led to it.

A final story here…

While I was developing FriendlyFriday I was in town one evening and needed something to eat. I went into a restaurant in Covent Garden and asked for a table for one. I was told there was nothing available but, as I was leaving, saw a couple come in who asked for a table and were seated at once.

I was really frustrated by this. Not only was it rude, but it felt like it bordered on discrimination by choosing not to serve someone simply because they were on their own. I understand as well as anyone the need to manage your business profitably, but this felt like a personal insult and a missed opportunity.

With my mind already bursting with ideas of connections, collisions and serendipity, I came up with a new related idea I called "Shareatable". London chain Le Pain Quotidien has a communal sharing table in many of its branches. Wagamama has long benches. Why not, therefore, take this a step further and invite restaurants to offer single diners the chance to share a table?

It would mean the restaurant wouldn't need to turn away business and could make more money by ensuring single diners didn't take up larger tables. It would also give the diners the chance to make a new connection and be more sociable. It might even encourage people to eat out more if they were on their own and otherwise didn't want to.

As I was pondering this idea, I wondered if maybe it would make sense to create something that would enable lone diners to meet up in advance and decide which restaurant

The Collision Code

to go to together, but I was drawn by the fact that restaurants offering this as a service would help them create a new customer base too. It felt foolproof!

I contacted lots of restaurant chains and pitched them the idea, but the response was lukewarm at best. Eventually, Wahaca in Kentish Town agreed to do a trial. It helped that I was a regular visiting and living locally, but I was excited someone was open to the idea.

> **ShareaTable** @shareatable · Jul 12, 2015
>
> Fancy Mexican but don't want2 eat alone? Go2 @wahaca #kentishtown after 5pm ask4 a table 4 1 & they'll do the rest
>
> 💬 2 🔁 6 ♡ 4 ⬆️

With everything set up, I wanted to test the concept for myself. I arrived at Wahaca and asked for a table for one, and right on cue I was asked if I wanted a "sharing table". Great! However, it seemed I was rumbled straight away as the staff member knew who I was and seemed to think I was testing her. At any rate, I sat at a table for four, ordered my food and waited to see what happened.

A few groups came in and then, soon after, the next solo person arrived.

The waitress asked him if he'd like to sit on a shared table and pointed over at me. He looked over, paused and shook his head. And that was it! I finished my meal alone and the trial ended a few weeks after that.

It was disappointing. I had imagined that the option to share would be out of sight of the sharing table itself so instead of seeing who you might be sharing with, you'd make that decision in advance. It felt like I'd been judged as not being worthy to share with, and that maybe if someone else had been there, he might have agreed.

Of course, I'm sure it wasn't me and that man just wanted to sit by himself. In addition, the restaurant was barely a quarter full at the time, so it probably didn't make any sense. I still believe some incarnation of this idea has legs, but for me it was a short-lived project to test out my thinking around collisions and how we get more people interacting in different ways.

As with anything, it's hard to anticipate all the challenges in advance until you give it a go. But that's not a reason not to get stuck in. New ideas take many iterations to get them right, but the only way to end up with something wonderful is to start with something a bit shaky.

Reflection Time: How can you create opportunities for connection in your own life, and what small actions can you take to encourage conversations with others?

Jazz FM and ?WhatIf!

I was approached by Elliot Moss from Mishcon de Reya, a law firm who were running a series of podcasts of interviews of businesspeople on Jazz FM's programme, Jazz Shapers.

I turned up to be recorded for the interview and all went smoothly. After my interview Elliot was recording another show with Matt Kingdon. Matt was the founder of ?WhatIf!, an innovation and marketing agency that I had followed since my late teens and was a huge admirer of their work so it was great to meet him.

We chatted about his book *Sticky Wisdom*, which I had read and he gave me a copy of his latest book *The Science of Serendipity: How to Unlock the Promise of Innovation in Large Organisations*.

The book gave the background and science behind everything I was trying to achieve through FriendlyFriday at the time and then going forward with Shareatable and Causr.

I reached out to him after I read the book and shared my FriendlyFriday story. He agreed to support me and provide some copies of his book I could give away as part of my FriendlyFriday presentation talking about connectivity and innovation. All very much continuing to lay the foundations for *The Collision Code*.

Mykonos Solo Dinner and Sunset Drinks

Back in 2018 I ended up living in Mykonos which you'll find out more about later. Every year since I've visited and to help people connect with each other I created Mykonos Solo Travellers & Friends which now has over 2,000 members. I put together a map with all my recommendations (https://www.bit.ly/MykonosbyJames) which has since been viewed over 9,000 times. When I'm visiting I often try to host a meal or get together and September 2024 was no exception. As I met people on the beach or in the bar or through friends I simply mentioned and suggested that I was going to host a drinks and dinner later in the week at a beautiful hotel overlooking the old town with an infinity pool and sunset view.

Six people were due to arrive, including one from France who was living in Switzerland, one from the UK, a publicist living in California, someone in finance living in West Hampstead just ten minutes from me in London. One person dropped out last minute so I put on my dating profile app that I was hosting a dinner and a few minutes later someone messaged me asking if they could join. It was exactly how I thought Causr would work (again, more on that later) but it's the recipe for everything we are talking about—this time technology enabled giving this person the permission, confidence and context to connect and meet. Most of the time on these apps people just waste their time talking and never actually making an in-person connection. But here we were. The feedback from the others at the dinner was that it was the best evening of their trip: beautiful sunset view, delicious food, amazing people, creating meaningful and genuine connections. It led to me changing my flights to stay an extra night in Mykonos and having the most magical end to almost a month of travelling (and working) "alone" in Greece.

Movie Moments

As you've journeyed through these stories, especially the most recent one, you may have sensed a recurring theme: the idea of movie moments. These are the flashes of magic, the moments that feel almost cinematic—unexpected, transformative and etched into memory. In the blur of daily life, where hours stretch into days, weeks into months, and years seem to pass in a blink, it's these highlights we carry with us forever. Movie moments often begin with anticipation, uncertainty and even hesitation. They're the times when we step outside our comfort zones—walking into a bar alone, setting off on a solo trip or simply daring to embrace the unknown.

Part II Making Connections

Emilia & James at Lola Bar in Mykonos

At the end of my trip to Mykonos, I found myself in one of those moments. Tired, drained from the constant motion, I almost gave in to the temptation to stay in. I called my friend Nick, sharing that I didn't have the energy to go out, that I was weary of pushing myself to make an effort. With a little nudge from him, I decided to go anyway. That's how I ended up at the charming little bar called Lola, where everything changed. (You'll read more about Lola later!)

Just minutes after walking in, I found myself striking up a conversation with Emilia, a vibrant woman wearing a sequin top and skirt covered in hearts that radiated the same energy she did. As we talked, the surface-level chatter gave way to something deeper. When I complimented her incredible energy, she confided in me about a health challenge she had been facing. That vulnerability opened a door, and I too shared a personal story—my own heart, both metaphorically and in connection with the dress she wore.

What followed was pure magic. We drank, we danced, we connected in a way that felt effortless yet profound. In that moment, two strangers became friends, all from a simple hello and a willingness to be open, raw and real. That night was a movie moment, complete with laughter, shared vulnerability and a photograph that captured the beginning of a new friendship.

These moments don't require grand gestures. They happen when we let down our walls, embrace serendipity and lean into the unpredictability of life. They are everywhere, waiting to unfold.

Reflection Time: What can you do each day to create more movie moments? What small acts of courage, openness or connection could lead to the next unforgettable scene in the movie of your life?

Going Places

I've always loved the idea of car sharing. It makes sense for the environment, congestion on the roads and it also saves money. Most of all, however, I like the idea of using it as a way to meet interesting people. So when I learnt about BlaBlaCar I was eager to sign up.

It's a pretty simple concept, effectively a marketplace for drivers and passengers. You enter a journey you are making and charge for a seat on the journey. Passengers can then book into journeys just as they would any other transport.

I was driving to Bristol for a friend's party and to see my younger brother for his birthday. With train prices at nearly £60 for the journey, I decided to drive and listed my journey on BlaBlaCar. Within twenty-four hours I got a booking for three people.

At the time, I drove a Mini, so I thought it would be tight. I was also a little concerned these were "unverified passengers" (like many systems, BlaBlaCar invites users to verify their identity with ID to ensure everyone's safety), but I made the decision to meet them at the pick-up point and, if I felt at all uncomfortable, decline to take them. When I arrived at Kentish Town tube station to meet them, I spotted a man and two women waiting. I got out, introduced myself, reassured myself that all was OK, and were good to go.

As we set off, the man, who had seated himself in the back, told me he had a condition that means he always falls asleep in moving vehicles. I joked that this sounded more of a gift than anything, but he was able to quietly excuse himself from the conversation and it was the last we heard of him.

Throughout the rest of the journey I spoke with the two women about life in general. Student Beans came up at one point and Priscila, who had booked the journey, mentioned she'd used it when she was studying. It's always lovely to hear that even after all these years.

The conversation soon turned to why they wanted to get to Bristol. It turned out they were going to the Banksy exhibition "Dismaland" in Weston-super-Mare. It was something I'd been interested in myself, but it had sold out quickly with tickets changing hands for up to £1,000 on the resale market. So when they offered me three spare tickets they had for Sunday I was quite taken aback. I was even more taken aback when they gave them to me for free! I was able to share them with my brother and his girlfriend and we had an amazing day out.

Weekend done, I had managed to secure another booking to take some people back to London from Bristol. As we drove through Sunday evening the conversation again turned to what we did. In the front was Hugo who worked in insurance. In the back was Pag, a firefighter, and his partner. I asked them, "If you could do anything, what would you do?" Everyone agreed it would be fun to get a boat and just spend time sailing around the world. But when they asked me directly, I said I'd just be doing exactly what I do now.

At this point I knew I was on the brink of something and I was excited about launching a new idea, Causr. But we'll get to that. Because I want to share a few more travel experiences with you first.

*　*　*

It was 4 a.m. and I was at Kentish Town train station to get myself to Gatwick Airport. The previous train had been cancelled and two other people were waiting with luggage. On the information board the message switched from "Delayed by a few minutes" to simply "Delayed". It didn't look good. Looking at the National Rail app all signs pointed to the train being cancelled too with the next not due for an hour. I could either get a taxi to Gatwick, or make my way to Victoria to get the Gatwick Express.

By now, you'll guess that I approached the others on the platform who had luggage with them to ask if they wanted to share an Uber with me (having confirmed they were also trying to make it to Gatwick). The cost worked out to be about the same as our train tickets and in the end we got to Gatwick about the same time and for the same money. But it took some initiative. The train destination and baggage

The Collision Code

they had provided clear context, while the train cancellation promoted urgency that can be so useful in finding the confidence to ask the question. As a result, my fellow passengers were pleased I'd taken the permission to engage them and all went well.

When things don't go to plan it's easy to just focus on your own issue. But sometimes combining forces and grouping together can help you and others.

Having told this story to my dad, some years later he phoned me up and told me this story in return...

He was working up in Newcastle and was making his way back to London when the train stopped in Milton Keynes. There had been a fatality on the tracks and all trains had been stopped. There was no clear indication of when they might start up again.

As Dad sat there on a Friday afternoon, after a lengthy trip away, he was keen to get home and see the family (more so given the circumstances of the delay). And so he asked himself, "What would James do?" And he did this...

Without much thought, as he told me, he stood up and told his section of the train that he was getting off and getting a taxi back to North London. If anyone wanted to join him, they were welcome. At first, of course, he got the usual silence and awkward stares. He felt a bit embarrassed, but he was there now. Within seconds, however, two women travelling together put up their hands and then they all went off.

During the hour-long journey the conversation flowed and Dad asked where they were headed. He knew it was to Golders Green, but they were more specific this time: "Middleway".

That was a coincidence as we used to live on that road, though Dad didn't think much of it. But when the taxi driver asked, "Which number?" his mouth fell open in disbelief. The house they were going to was a house he used to own. It was the house I spent the first five years of my life in. It was now owned by one of the women's grandmothers and they invited him in for a look before he walked home.

What are the chances? Slim, of course. But not as slim as they would be by not ever taking a chance to make that particular collision at all.

I was so thrilled to see my dad making this leap. But it's just one example of the potentially millions of missed connections and opportunities that might be out there if we were only to collide into each other a bit more often; to take the chance to talk and connect and connect.

* * *

On another occasion, I had been invited to a friend's wedding in Inverness.

On the day of my flight some major building works had held up my journey to the airport. Fortunately I made it to the departure gate in time for the flight but another friend, Andrew, wasn't so lucky. We had agreed to meet at the airport and then share a taxi at the other end as the venue was quite some distance from the airport. As I couldn't see him in the departure lounge, I messaged to find he was still stuck in traffic while we were boarding.

Indeed, on the plane it was clear a lot of people were missing, no doubt all for the same reason. For Andrew's part he ended up parking in Luton and rushing to Heathrow for another flight to try to make the wedding in time. As for me, I was on the flight without a travel buddy and facing a solo taxi journey that would cost far more than the flight itself.

After take-off I decided to walk up the plane to see if I knew or recognised anyone else who might be going to the wedding. I didn't, but I did spot something else—someone wearing a kippah (a Jewish head covering). As this was a Jewish wedding I asked if he happened to be on his way to Guy and Gabi's celebration and it turned out he was. In fact, he was part of the wedding band. This meant his travel was all sorted with various instruments and tech to transport too.

I hatched another plan. I spoke to the cabin crew and explained my dilemma. I asked if they would be willing to make an announcement to see if anyone else was attending the wedding. She kindly agreed to do just that, and straight away five hands shot up at the front of the plane. I made my way down and we all agreed to share cars after landing. What a relief.

In the end, one of the passengers in the taxi was close to the family of the bride and refused to let anyone else pay for the journey. So from an expensive taxi fare, to a free one, just for asking the question. But that wasn't the best of it.

On the taxi journey I chatted to an older couple who lived in Vienna, as it happens exactly where my grandparents came from before moving to the UK. For years we'd said we'd visit as a family but had never got round to it. After the wedding I set in motion plans for a trip with my dad, brothers and sister to visit Vienna together on what would have been my grandfather's one hundredth birthday. Without that chance meeting it probably wouldn't have happened.

While I note it's not practical for the cabin crew to make an announcement for every passenger who might want to grab a lift, I'm glad I asked. And as in every situation, the cabin crew—or whoever else is in charge—are usually people who want to help out where they can.

That said, it wasn't my first rodeo...

In 2010, three of my friends were travelling to Nice for a few days. Due to work commitments I was only able to join them for the last couple of days of the trip but was still keen to fly out.

As the dates drew near, French Air Traffic Control announced they would strike and so all flights to Nice were cancelled. The only other airport that was relatively nearby, and open, was Genoa in Italy (around a three-hour drive, or a ten-hour train journey). But, of course, me with my ever-positive mindset figured that there must be other people in the same situation and I'd be able to work it out.

I boarded the plane to Genoa with absolutely no idea how I was going to get to Nice!

As soon as we were airborne, I started to ask around to see if anybody else might be going to Nice. I started with the person next to me, of course, but no luck. Then I asked the cabin crew if they'd be willing to make an announcement. They were, and they asked anyone who was looking to make their way to Nice to press the "call button" at their seat.

Ping. Ping. Ping. Ping. In the end nine or so lights went on and, over the next hour, I traversed the plane exchanging stories and starting to work out what to do next.

A few were adamant they would get the train, others were keen to try to find a taxi. I narrowed the groups down to two couples, one from New Zealand trying to get to Nice, and another from the UK actually trying to get to Monaco for a wedding. As we landed nothing concrete had been agreed but I'd floated the idea of renting a car we could all use.

Part II Making Connections

As I only had hand luggage I raced to the car hire companies to try to beat the rush. The first company I spoke to, Europcar, wanted to charge €300 for a half hay rental as the drop off in Nice counted as an "international" trip. Others didn't have cars available. As it had been a very expensive trip already, what with the strikes and changes, I went back to Europcar to explain the predicament and see what they could do.

After a few taps on the computer they were able to offer a car for €210. It always helps to ask.

Now with keys in hand, I waited for the other couples to tell them I could drive them if they were happy to split the costs. Within twenty minutes of landing, five of us were in the car and heading off towards Monte Carlo.

Two hours into the journey, I started to panic. I hadn't seen any signs that suggested we were going the right way for quite some time, but I reasoned that as long as the sea was on our left we must be heading in the right direction. As the road turned inland, however, I got a little more nervous, so I was pleased to see a sign to Monaco just a few miles up the road. I didn't know what I'd say to my passengers if I'd inadvertently taken them to Switzerland. Maybe when you've chosen to trust your gut, you've got to keep believing in it!

I dropped off the first couple in Monaco and we drove on, arriving at Nice airport in just under three hours. I filled the car with petrol just before arrival and with tolls, petrol and rental the total came to €230. As the others had agreed to pay €60 each, I actually ended up with a free trip and €10 for a welcome drink on arrival.

A few weeks later, the trip a mere memory, I got an email into the Student Beans enquiry account. On the journey we must have discussed some business because the message read: "Hi there, this is a message for James to thank him very much for the lift from Genoa to Monte Carlo and just wondering what the accounting software he mentioned was. Cheers, Chris Wilson."

It's a tiny thing, but it always fascinates me what these collisions turn up (and I was glad to recommend things I've found useful!).

As a final word on airports, I once had a chance encounter with the great Rory Sutherland while flying back from the Netherlands. If you're not aware of him, Rory is an advertising guru who is the vice-chair of Ogilvy and Mather. He had written several books on advertising, brands and behavioural science and is something of a legend in certain circles.

I had never met Rory before in person, but I did think I had enough in my "layers of connection" to strike up a chat. I knew he'd been invited to speak at Voxburner events before (part of Student Beans) which gave me the context to give myself permission to say hello. After all, what did I have to lose?

We spoke for some time as our flights were delayed and covered a whole range of subject matter from manufacturing serendipity to my new idea Causr (more on which is coming very soon). He shared some really interesting insights and it was great to hear his take on the things I was thinking deeply about.

Another day, another collision. But when it's someone you admire, it's easy to be a little starstruck. The thing is, if you don't know them personally, you probably have some context with which to approach them to say hello. If it's polite enough and interesting enough, you don't know where it could lead. In this case, at the time an inspiring conversation, that's more than enough. More recently as I shared this story with Rory he kindly provided an endorsement for this book:

You can't control luck. What you can control is your odds of getting lucky. With practical wisdom and relatable stories, *The Collision Code* is an essential read for anyone looking to unlock the potential of everyday moments and manufacture serendipity.

Rory Sutherland, Vice Chairman of Ogilvy, Author of Alchemy

On which note, let me finally tell you about Causr.

Reflection Time: How can embracing unexpected connections and opportunities in our everyday travels enhance our experiences and lead to meaningful interactions with others?

Where It's At

For a while I'd been interested in how *where* we are, as well as *who* we are, can be a factor in making collisions. It seems obvious, but in our increasingly technology-driven lives it's often the case that we work with (and even socialise with) people we might never have met in person. Meanwhile, in any public space we might be sitting right next to someone we have something in common with, but never know.

At the start of 2014 I moved into a flat in a converted school in Kentish Town. As I settled into the building I couldn't help but notice how quiet it was, despite there being twenty-five flats in total, and mostly long-standing residents.

I thought of hosting a drinks party to introduce myself, but as so often happens the days turned into weeks and the weeks into months and I hadn't done anything. By then it was nearly Christmas so I invited everyone in the building to the local pub and was pleased that ten or so flats turned up. It was great fun, and everyone said they'd hardly met anyone else in the building before.

Building on this, I thought it would be a good idea to create a WhatsApp group. So, one evening I knocked on every door inviting people to join. I told them that everyone else had already signed up, which to begin with wasn't true, of course, but then nobody felt they had to go first. Soon everyone was in a group and it's proved to be a huge success.

Here are just some of the things the group has helped make happen:

- a loan of a freezer space when someone's freezer stopped working
- help jump starting a car due to a dead battery
- advice on how to get rid of moths
- organisation of people borrowing designated car park spaces for family/friends
- complaints when there was too much noise during a party (leading to cupcakes being left for everyone the following day)
- identifying whether an infestation was bees or wasps
- a Halloween drinks flat crawl
- film screenings and lots of ticket exchanges for gigs and events
- computer help and access to a printer

When a couple had a new baby, one of the other residents even hosted their mother for a visit as they had a spare room. And during a power cut there was only the need to make one phone call to the power company in order to update everyone on what was happening.

When people move out there is now a handover process to the new owners or tenants to make sure they are included in the group. The community has been transformed and you get a sense that people who felt alone and anonymous in their own building now have other people who look out and care for them.

Living in the same place is the most obvious and simple form of context that can build a sense of connection and community, and with very little effort. If you don't already have a group on WhatsApp or email for your building or street, why not start one? (See the appendix for a "how to" guide.)

* * *

I'd first been drawn to Kentish Town in 2014 when looking for new offices for Student Beans. We felt that being out in Golders Green was limiting our ability to attract talent and had originally looked around "Silicon Roundabout" near Old Street, but the rents were excruciating and we were wary of buying into the hype.

Titus Sharpe, a founder of MVF Global, was speaking alongside me at an event in Oxford and mentioned that their offices were in Kentish Town. This planted a seed, and I went to look at Highgate Studios which we moved into just a few months later. The rent was reasonable and it was much more accessible than Golders Green.

A short while later I was being interviewed by Julian Blake from Tech City Insider as part of the Almanac 2014 series. In chatting I mentioned I wanted to do something for the community in and around Kentish Town now we'd set roots there. Julian introduced me to Tom Kihl from *The Kentish Towner* magazine and together with other local luminaries

Zoe Cunningham of Softwire, Justine Roberts of Mumsnet, and Titus Sharpe too, we launched Kentish Cluster. The aim was, as it always is, to bring the community together by creating more collisions.

Over the years Kentish Cluster ran a whole range of initiatives from round table discussions for business leaders to monthly drinks meet-ups at a different venue each month. We got sponsorship from landlords to help fund the first drink and regularly had thirty to forty people turning up who all lived or worked in the area.

On one visit back to my student roots at the University of Birmingham the visit coincided with the Conservative Party conference. During an event I was speaking at, I ended up being introduced to one of the prime minister's special advisers and found myself talking about the growth opportunities around Kentish Town and, by extension, the work I'd done on Kentish Cluster. It turned out the adviser lived locally and he suggested a round table at Downing Street to discuss the opportunities with a group of local business leaders. It's funny to think I had to go all the way to Birmingham to make the connection and make something so prestigious happen. But that's often how these things work.

By having something community based and neutral (with Student Beans involved by default as it's where our offices were), I had a different context to start a conversation that wasn't primarily about sales, but about community. It felt so freeing to just connect with people and see if any opportunities emerged. I knew if I'd contacted the landlord and pubs as Student Beans, for example, they would have been less accommodating or wouldn't even entertain a conversation.

Kentish Cluster Members outside 10 Downing Street

Similarly, had I just connected with the PM's advisor focusing just on Student Beans I don't think we could have gained the invite to Downing Street.

The glue of the local community also made for a ready-built context for any conversation. It's very easy to start chatting to someone when you can ask where they live or work as a starting point (and, of course, have the permission to do so!).

All of which I had in mind in 2016 when I started to think seriously about the business that would become Causr.

If you're interested in setting up your own "cluster" or community, there's a guide in the appendix.

Reflection Time: In what ways can you take initiative to create meaningful connections and foster community in your own neighbourhoods or workplaces, and what impact might that have on your personal and professional life?

Causr

I'd been at Student Beans day to day for over ten years. We built the business from scratch without any investment aside from The Prince's Trust—it was a huge achievement. I loved what we created but appreciated that starting a business and running one are two very different things. I had to be honest where I was at. Michael, my co-founder and brother, was always the one who knew how to get things done, taking on the operational side of the business. Simon, my eldest brother, had joined the company about three years earlier, stepping into the role of commercial director after I left the position. Along with William (our seventh employee who later spearheaded our launch in the US) and Vincent our CTO, the four of them, together with other key team members, gave me the confidence to step away from the day-to-day operations. Though I knew challenges lay ahead, I felt assured the business was in more than capable hands. I will be forever grateful for the work they and all the team have done over the years knowing the sacrifices they have made and what it takes to build and grow something from nothing. The creation of Student Beans with Michael is still one of my greatest legacies and it wouldn't have been possible without him.

You may recall that when I read *The Naked Leader* back in 2003 it invited me, as with all readers, to imagine what would happen if I couldn't fail. That had led me to launch Student Beans based on an idea I'd had that just seemed unstoppable. When I came up with the idea for Causr, it felt exactly the same.

In 2014 Michael and I were selected as two of startups. co.uk's annual "Young Guns", a network for burgeoning talent in the sector. It was through this network that I met an investor interested in Student Beans and it was over lunch with this investor that I shared the initial idea of getting people to share tables in restaurants, and later my idea for Causr. Over time this investor said they were interested in supporting the venture, but that I had to be working on this idea full time and no longer be involved in Student Beans day to day. This was the final push I needed to make the difficult, yet necessary, decision to move to the next chapter of my life.

My mission by now was very simple: make millions of connections for people nearby, all around the world, every day.

Part II Making Connections

From the stories I've been sharing in these past chapters you can see the foundations of this idea, but for the idea to scale I figured it needed a technological solution. I thought it needed an app.

After I created a clickable PowerPoint of what I wanted and how it should work, I built a very basic version of what I wanted to create with a coding school who helped me test the concept whilst I got our first users and tested messaging.

The app would work like this. People could sign up and create a profile logging in with LinkedIn, after which they'd be directed to select from a number of dedicated groups. Being a member of these groups would show you who else in that group was nearby. So groups might be created for alumni from a specific university, or for colleagues from a particular business, or even those working in the same industry. But it could also be for fans of a sports team, or owners of a certain car or anything else really. However, business and networking benefits were what I felt would be the driver of the app as a commercial offering. People do business with people and the logic was that if we could provide useful context and more physical connections for people to make more and more collisions, then we could become a really valuable part of people's lives.

Or to put it another way, Causr was designed to create the context and permission that would give people confidence to make more collisions. I was truly excited about its potential.

It is now often said we are more (digitally) connected than ever before at the same time more disconnected, isolated and lonely than we ever have been. My belief around Causr was that technology could be used to create more offline connections. The technology was the enabler.

Of course, with any idea like this, it lives or dies by how many users you can get. I tried using Facebook and Twitter ads, but the costs were too high and we weren't getting repeat users. My original and main aim was to always focus on building a base through organisations and existing communities.

Early on I met with a private members club in London who were really interested in the idea, but felt that being iOS only (as it was at that stage) was a real limitation. I began exploring how we could make an Android version available so organisations would find it easy to look past any of the technological barriers.

I saw three very clear benefits of Causr that I used in my pitch to organisations:

1. Cost saving: If people can connect more easily in a physical place, then they can, for example, car share or split taxi fares.
2. Improved wellbeing: Being more connected, more of the time, makes people feel less isolated and alone.

3. More opportunities: By creating all these collisions over and over, the potential for new business, new friendships and other opportunities increases exponentially.

I thought things were going well. I had all the investment lined up.

Then "Terrible Tuesday" hit.

At the start of this adventure I'd brought a technical co-founder on board and engaged a number of investors to help get things off the ground. Just as things were looking like maybe something might happen, one of the investors dropped out when their personal circumstance changed. That same day the technical co-founder decided he didn't want to pursue Causr full time. He was happy to be an advisor, but no more. I was crestfallen.

Among various frustrations was the fact I'd applied for the SEIS scheme. It's a government-backed scheme that gives tax relief on investments and therefore makes investment much more attractive. It was taking a long time to come through and it felt that had created a window through which investment and technical expertise was escaping.

But what can you do but crack on? I buckled down and within a month I had some more investment secured and had chosen an agency in Bristol to work on the app. Things were moving forward and I was feeling optimistic again.

The Collision Code

We got some good press coverage and Sir Richard Branson himself even highlighted us in a post on LinkedIn.

> **Richard Branson** in**fluencer** — 2mth
> Founder at Virgin Group
>
> Technology should enable more in-person interactions, not reduce them. Good example here:
>
> **This entrepreneur has invented a new way of networking - would you use it?**
> virgin.com · That's what made James Eder, founder of Causr (which we'll talk more about in a minute), create hi...
>
> Unlike · Comment · Share · 👍 1264 💬 50
>
> Show previous comments
>
> Michelle Morgan Nice one James — 1mth
> Unlike · Reply · 👍 you
>
> Gail Thomas Yes I agree — 1mth
> Unlike · Reply · 👍 you
>
> Add a comment...
>
> See all updates ›

We managed to build our user base to 3,000 users, but we couldn't get any organisations to sign on. I initially tried offering free trials to people, but that didn't work. So I offered paid trials (sometimes it helps to show the value of something to have a price on it), but it wasn't a big enough requirement for people and I just couldn't get any commitments.

Still, I persevered and kept having conversations while the Android app was developed. I knew that if I could just keep going, something would happen. There were a few wins, of course. My old school agreed to promote Causr to alumni, and The Prince's Trust pushed it to their network too. But the response was underwhelming and disappointing. While I had a clear vision of the outcomes, somehow nobody else could seem to see it. It was frustrating to say the least.

In January 2017 I set about connecting with over 1,000 technical types to see if I could find someone to bring on board and make Causr a really serious proposition in the tech space. I contacted CTOs, lead developers and anyone I thought might lead me to the right people, just making collisions left, right and centre every hour of every day both online and at events. Through all that I made a shortlist of ten people or organisations I felt could help.

Speaking to them all, things really clicked with Oleg who had been looking for something but not found a mission that resonated with him. This did. I was thrilled. We agreed on a package of salary and options that I could meet once the next round of funding came in. In the meantime, he agreed to help build out the much-needed Android version of the app which was taking place in Moldova. We figured that would give us a chance to work together and ensure the partnership was solid. He cracked on building things and I tried to bring more people on board.

Life, of course, is never simple. But it got particularly complicated for me in June 2017 as things were really hitting a crunch point. That's a much bigger story for the next chapter, but suffice to say, I still believed in Causr and wasn't go-

The Collision Code

ing to let anything slow things down. I still went to events, I spoke at conferences and I met with as many people as I could. I was determined to make Causr happen.

And then, as the wheels wobbled, they threatened to come off completely when the latest CTO decided that Causr wasn't for him. This was incredibly disappointing after all the work I'd done, and the potential I felt we had to do something brilliant. Moreover, it was before the Android development was complete so I now had that on my plate too. I took over management of the developers and we pushed on. Again, what else could I do?

Android app in hand, I went back to the communities who'd cited that as an issue in earlier conversation. Not one of them was willing to take the leap, even with this resolved. It was beyond frustrating. But still... I kept going.

* * *

During this time, I spoke at a Lean Startup event in London. Part of the event was a pitch competition to win a ticket for their event in San Francisco with Eric Ries, author of *The Lean Startup* itself. It was an opportunity to grab, so whatever else was going on, I reached right towards it and managed to get my hands on it. I was off to San Francisco.

One morning, before the conference started, I had time so I walked around San Francisco's streets. I found myself on

Market Street and fancied a drink, so went into Joe & The Juice and found a comfy spot. Looking around, I was surrounded by people on their laptops. I wondered, as I always do, what they were doing and what they might be creating.

Some code flashed up on the screen next to me. I pounced.

"Do you mind if I ask you a question? I saw the code on your screen." Context. I was wary, as interrupting someone in that environment is always a little presumptuous, but I always figure if the response is anything but completely friendly you can just be brief and make it easy for them to exit the conversation.

On this occasion, I got a friendly response. "Sure!"

I introduced myself and explained I'd travelled from London. It turned out so had he. He was Dennis, co-founder and CTO of Flexciton. I said I was in town for Lean Startup week and was trying to find a technical co-founder for Causr. He recognised the problem we were trying to solve straight away. He'd been at the conference too, but found it hard to meet anyone relevant with over 4,000 people attending.

As we chatted, Dennis mentioned he was part of the Entrepreneur First community. I had met one of the founders, Matt Clifford, some time ago and had met with the team at their office just the week before. I fired up Causr and showed him the "Entrepreneurs First" group on the app.

The Collision Code

The idea was if you clicked on the Entrepreneurs First group you could see who else from the community was nearby, giving you the context to connect to them (of course, this was dependent on them having the app installed and being a Causr user).

It didn't go further than that, but it was a good chat and it instilled more confidence in me that good people with similar intentions are out there just waiting to collide with each other.

Work finished, it made sense to spend some time enjoying the city and so my partner at the time, Michael, flew out to meet me. We looked up a community called OneTable.org that hosts Jewish Friday night dinners across the US (and beyond), and found a host to meet some new people in town. It was a "bring a dish" situation, and we were welcomed with open arms as we arrived with some drinks.

As part of the dinner, the host, Christine, circulated a pack of cards containing various questions that would help stimulate conversation. It was a lovely idea to really deepen the connection between everyone. To make it nice and accessible, you could choose to answer a card or pass and pick a new one, so nobody was forced to feel uncomfortable or at a loss of what to say. I also loved it because it created permission for people to share, and gave context to bring up stories and thoughts that might otherwise never have been shared.

Long ago, this seemed to be something that happened in coffee houses and pubs around the world, where ideas were shared and discussed and minds broadened. In the modern age, as we do so much online and are led so much by algorithms, we somehow seem to have dulled this thirst for really knowing others, replacing it with an obsession for the newest, shiniest, most shocking "content". Making these connections at random times has always really nourished my soul, and it is sad that it's the exception—requiring hard work and breaking social convention to achieve—rather than the rule.

* * *

When I returned from San Francisco I kept contacting people and trying to make things work with Causr but there were no big wins before the end of the year.

And on that note, let me tell you what happened in June 2017.

Reflection Time: In what ways do your surroundings and the communities you are part of influence your opportunities for connection and collaboration, and how can you actively enhance these relationships in your own life?

My Heart

The day 19 June 2017 was just like any other day. I was in the Netherlands and visiting my partner for a friends wed-

The Collision Code

ding. It was a fun weekend at the start of the summer and so, we decided to go to a theme park. Our plan was to go on a few gentler rides first, before ratcheting things up a bit with the G-Force roller coaster. The name gives you some idea of what we were hoping to experience.

After walking around the park in the morning sun, we headed for the log flume. Having splashed down, I jumped out of the large replica log and skipped out of the way of the next group careering through the water, keen to avoid getting soaked.

As I went to run up the steps and away from the ride, I felt a sudden loss of strength in my legs. I tried to grab the handrail but I wasn't able to support my own weight. My knees gave way, and I fell to the floor. Slumping backwards, my head came into contact with the floor and I was momentarily knocked unconscious.

When I came round a few seconds later, I felt utterly confused. Where was I? What was going on? It was like that scene in *The Matrix* where Switch and the others are still inside, but have been unplugged from the chair. I didn't feel right, but I didn't know why.

We found somewhere to sit and I had some water and food, and we decided that we would leave the theme park. The rest of the day I felt better, but a little lightheaded. As we pottered around the coast and spent time in the shade, every time I felt my body not quite responding as I'd want,

I wondered what might be going on. I pushed on, and flew home to the UK that evening as planned.

But I can't say I wasn't a little concerned.

As soon as I got back to London I went to see my doctor. My GP noted my blood pressure was a bit low when I stood up compared to sitting down, so he suggested I go get an ECG and some blood tests.

Assuming this was just a very routine check-up, I arrived for my tests, and parked in a pay and display car park paying for one hour. I checked in and was quickly seen and given an ECG (an echocardiogram, a simple test to check how your heart is operating). As the results came through the nurse disappeared and returned shortly after with the consultant.

"Does anyone in your family have a heart condition?"

"No, I don't think so."

"Has a relative ever died very suddenly?"

"No, I don't think so."

The doctor nodded and told me I needed to have an ultrasound scan of my heart and to cancel any plans I had for the rest of the day. Within minutes they took my blood and carried out the ultrasound which was immediately reviewed by a specialist.

By now it was obvious that there was something to be concerned about, and I was told there appeared to be an abnormality in my heart that might have caused my episode at the water park. I was told I would have to stay in the hospital.

There were a lot of thoughts that whirred through my head, but the first was, *Can I move my car?* Having only paid for an hour, and with all this going on, I didn't want the hassle of dealing with a parking ticket on top of everything that was going on. The doctors agreed but said I had to come straight back and to report to A&E when I did.

On the short drive home I was in shock. I packed a bag and got a taxi straight back to the hospital, finding time to call my family on the way.

Lying in my hospital bed I could see the BT Tower, a tall column-like building that looms over central London. Just a few weeks before I'd been to an event there. It has a revolving events space at the top with quite spectacular views of the city. And here I was looking out at it from a corner of London I never thought I'd find myself in. Who does?

The person opposite me in the hospital ward was recovering from a stroke and learning how to both walk and speak again. The two others were much older gentlemen; the kind of people you expect to find in hospital. As I looked at them fighting on at the end of their lives, I wondered what they thought of me being there.

A friend put things in perspective when they came to visit.

"If you're asking why this is happening to you… Why not?"

It was blunt. But it's true. It's always true. There is no typical patient.

I spent three days in hospital being monitored, having blood tests and being poured over by doctors looking for answers from my initial scans. On day three I was waiting to have an MRI scan (essentially a very detailed image of my heart) that might hold some clues.

"You need to stay as still as you can so we can get a good picture of your heart."

And there I was, in the machine, stuck. I couldn't go back. But I didn't know what might lay ahead.

I was scared. What would they find? What would it mean? How serious would it be?

At various stages of the scan I was told to breathe in, then breathe out, then to hold my breath. I noticed my hands begin to go numb and start to hurt. I daren't move. I didn't want to know. I just wanted to stop.

"OK, nearly done…"

I held my breath.

After the initial tests the results came through, they determined that I had hypertrophic cardiomyopathy (HCM).

This is a condition in which the wall of the heart has thickened, reducing the amount of blood the heart can pump. After being referred to a specialist at St Bartholomew's Hospital in central London, I spent the summer of 2017 having test after test, multiple scans and many consultations with different medical professionals. Eventually I was referred to Royal Papworth Hospital for review and to be considered for a heart transplant.

It was a challenging time. In fact, as I write this in 2024, it still is. Uncertainty is always hard.

At my flat in London I normally have a flatmate. Sometimes, in between the comings and goings, I have used Airbnb to fill the room. On 21 September 2017, after my initial meeting and being told I need to be referred to Papworth for a potential heart transplant and heart failure treatment, the next guest who booked into the room was in film production. While chatting I asked more about this and enquired what he was working on. He was in the process of finishing up a documentary celebrating the fiftieth anniversary of the world's first heart transplant.

Dr Christiaan Barnard, a South African surgeon, made history on 3 December 1967 when he and his team performed the world's first human heart transplant in Cape Town. This pioneering surgery paved the way for people like me to have hope of success should I need a new heart. Sometimes it's about timing. There simply was no hope before this breakthrough.

And what an example of serendipity. You can imagine how I was feeling at the time: vulnerable, anxious, full of questions. The enormity of a potential heart transplant was weighing heavily on me and I didn't know what to think. But sometimes things pop into your life when you most need them, like an Airbnb guest with a reminder of the work that has gone into giving people with heart conditions a better chance of survival.

This was a clear example.

Sometimes they're not so obvious.

But when I'm facing a hard time I always look out for something to lift me up. If the world can bring you down, it can lift you up too.

Reflective Time: In moments of uncertainty or fear in your life, what sources of hope or inspiration have you found, and how can you actively seek out or recognise these moments when facing future challenges?

Part III

Moving Forward

Mykonos

Having been diagnosed with hypertrophic cardiomyopathy, I remembered an old friend from AIESEC, Andrew Webster, who worked for the British Heart Foundation as its Head of Media. The charity is based just a mile from where I live so I got in touch with him and arranged to have lunch.

As we caught up and chatted, Andrew offered to introduce me to the person in charge of their cardiac nurse Heart Helpline. I'm sure they're just as approachable for anyone going through heart-related issues, but it was a welcome bit of support to have that connection to lean on. I've leant on their support a number of times over the years and it's been a real comfort.

One time was back in April 2018 when I'd just been told I was a good candidate for a heart transplant, but didn't need to have one immediately. The plan was to monitor me regularly and see where things stood, so I was booked in to come back in six months for more tests. One thing I'd already been told was having a heart transplant would require me to limit my exposure to the sun as the operation increases the risk of skin cancer. So I thought I'd book a holiday.

I booked to go to Mykonos in Greece, somewhere I'd always wanted to visit and was looking forward to heading out at the end of the month. However, before I left, my London specialist got in touch to tell me that, due to risks associated with my profile as a patient, they wanted to place an ICD (implantable cardioverter-defibrillator) in my body. There are different types but this would potentially regulate my heartbeat and, if there were any issues, use electrical shocks to try to restore a normal rhythm without any further intervention.

I was confused. Why hadn't this been mentioned when I'd been told about the potential of a transplant just weeks earlier? I spoke to various doctors and contacts to try to make sense of everything. Ultimately it was the permanence that I struggled with. I knew I needed to get this done, but somehow admitting to it made my condition real. The British Heart Foundation team was really amazing and so helpful at this time. They gave me information and support and talked me through my options.

That said, I was still determined to have my time in the sun. The operation would require several weeks of recovery and it seemed silly to waste the best months of the year, so I pushed the decision back with a view to have the ICD fitted towards the end of the year and flew out to Greece.

Part III Moving Forward

It was pre-season when I arrived and I meandered about the island on a moped exploring the white painted streets just trying to relax and enjoy the beautiful surroundings. One evening in a beautiful cocktail bar called Lola (mentioned in an earlier story where I met Emilia) I got talking to Edward, a fellow Brit who'd been in Mykonos for over thirty years. The conversation turned to the bustle of the summer season itself and, for some reason, I became fixated on the idea of getting a job and staying on the island. Sunshine, swimming, an escape from the day-to-day routine back home and a final hurrah before having this permanent marker of my heart condition all felt the right thing for me.

Edward introduced me to Sharon who owned a B&B that he'd first worked at when he came to the island. Villa Konstantin was just up from the old town with an incredible view of the sunset each night. I spoke to Sharon about me working there doing anything really, from reception to clearing rooms. An offer was made with pay and accommodation included. All that was in my diary was a wedding in July and so I agreed I would work the whole rest of the time from June through to September. She was happy, I was happy and that was that. I headed back to London and arrived a few weeks later with my bags and a big grin.

It didn't last long. At the end of my first day I phoned my partner in tears wondering what on earth I had done. The work was more basic than I had expected and I felt utterly overwhelmed by the commitment I had made to do this for three months. But after a pep talk, I did what you always have to do in these situations and got stuck in. Soon, I really started to enjoy the Greek way of life. Or at least tolerate it.

I shared a room with an older guy called Bernard and we got on well. I couldn't say the same for the receptionist who was in the next room, who had a very loud alarm set for 7 a.m. each morning. It would ring for thirty minutes nonstop after which she'd get up and turn it off. I asked her if it was possible to just set it for 7.30 a.m. but she refused and said there was no other way she was able to get up. I paused and thought, *OK, let's embrace that then.* After which I got up with the alarm each morning, drove to a nearby beach and had a swim (often more of a splash) before starting my own shift at 10 a.m. It was bliss.

My favourite part of the job was meeting guests and sharing my favourite tips about the island, such as where to eat or where to get a great view. The bar work was also fun, though I'd not worked in a bar for eighteen years so had to somewhat muddle through. Lorraine, a local bar owner, confided that as long as the drinks tasted of alcohol nobody would complain, so I stuck to that rule of thumb.

As the days went on, the first month raced by and I was soon off to my friend's wedding. I think Sharon was worried

I wouldn't return afterwards, but I was excited to. Island life was really growing on me. All that mattered was today, and maybe tomorrow. I never had to think about next week.

One of the other highlights of the summer was meeting Clémence who I'm still in touch with. She was the resident yoga instructor. Whilst I joined some classes, we did some one-to-one work and over the years have seen each other including continuing online classes. Always at the end of the phone she's one of those people who just wants to help.

Mykonos was just what I needed to make some space for myself among some life-changing challenges. And I'm glad I gave myself permission to do it. I'm so grateful to Sharon for trusting me and giving me the opportunity to escape for the summer and live the island life. It wasn't easy but looking back, it was I think one of the best things I could have done and will always remember summer 2018 in Mykonos.

* * *

One of my favourite things about living in Mykonos for a short time was the freedom to explore all the different restaurants and beaches on offer, especially the ones off the beaten track. At the beginning of July my partner Michael came to visit. Knowing that me choosing to move to Greece for three months was tough on him, I wanted to make sure his trip was perfect. And so, I planned where we'd go, what we'd do and where we'd eat with complete precision only opting for places I thought would offer a great experience.

For the last night of the trip I had booked a table at Funky Kitchen, a special little place hidden down a back street and literally behind a traditional Greek restaurant called Marco Polo. To actually enter Funky Kitchen you had to walk through Marco Polo, right past all the tables. Unless you knew it was there you'd never even find it. I'd not been, as when I'd last tried to come I'd been turned away as they were full. But since the Chocolate Nirvana Cake, among other things, was the talk of the town, I didn't want to miss out again.

On arrival we were welcomed by the hostess, Andrea, and our fabulous meal started with arancini risotto balls, olives and homemade bread followed by honey feta rolls with the most incredible marmalade sauce (far better than it sounds!). After that, I opted for the salmon while Michael had beef cheeks which melted like butter as he cut into them. For dessert, we tried the Chocolate Nirvana Cake everyone raved about along with a gorgeous crème caramel with homemade fresh mint ice cream. And all that was topped off with a homemade limoncello.

It was all sublime.

Throughout the evening, Andrea continued to serve and get to know us. We learnt she was the owner and, unsurprisingly, knew my boss Sharon. It was a brilliant evening and despite having travelled to most corners of the world and eaten in many wonderful places, I'd rate it as the best place I've ever had dinner.

After that night, Funky Kitchen became my number one recommendation for guests. Not a night went by that I didn't send someone there, and the pleasure I got the following day when guests returned with glowing feedback was just lovely. It's always a job to find something that's so consistently good that I knew nobody would be left disappointed.

The chef at Funky Kitchen, Pavlos, is married to Andrea. Along with her hospitality and easy manner, it's his attention to detail and clear passion for food that shines through. This joint labour of love was so inspiring to me, and I was overjoyed to keep sending people their way to help them succeed in doing what they love. Often I would recommend the restaurant to people on the beach before I started work, and I'd hear back from Andrea that someone had come in because they'd heard about it from a jolly Englishman at the beach!

Michael visited a couple more times while I was on Mykonos and we've been back to the island multiple times since that summer. We always ate at Funky Kitchen at least once until, unfortunately, it closed down. However, Pavlos continues to be a private chef on the island and at the time of writing could still be found on Airbnb Experiences. Andrea and Pavlos are now true friends for life and I'm so grateful for the hospitality they have shown me and hundreds of others I've sent them over the years.

Why am I telling you this? When you find something you love, it makes it so easy to want to share it. It creates a wonderfully valuable nugget of context you can use to start or continue a conversation. And in doing so, you gain in a very different way to when you're in "opportunity-seeking" mode. You help others, of course (in this case to find a nice place for dinner, or to support the business itself), but you also build a stronger connection with something that espouses the values you admire. And that can lead to friendship and the deeper human connection that brings with it.

But what I love even more about this story is that it presents collisions as something you can make happen. For you, for someone else you love, and for others. Collisions just pinging over and over adding more positivity and joy into the world and strengthening the connections between people, even if it's just two people who enjoy a special meal together. Whenever I would meet people randomly on the island I would often ask if they wanted any recommendations and Funky Kitchen was always first on the list.

Think about the businesses, places, people and works of art you really love and find so easy to recommend. Keep putting them out there.

Reflective Time: What are some passions or experiences in your life that bring you joy, and how can you share them with others to create meaningful connections and positive moments in your community?

Deep

Towards the end of my summer in Mykonos, I knew I needed to turn my mind back to whether I was going to get an ICD implanted that could save my life. In order to focus back on this, I reached out to the British Heart Foundation once more and they were able to introduce me to another young person who was willing to share his experience with me.

His story was a bit different from mine. He had collapsed at the gym and been rushed to hospital where his diagnosis was such that he was told he had to have an ICD there and then. Since it's been implanted, he told me, it has saved his life up to six times. On two of those occasions he was just lying asleep in bed, other times he was more active out and about or at the gym. Speaking to him and seeing the life that he was able to live, that might not otherwise have been the case, it was an easy decision. I was ready.

We talked more about the actual procedure and recovery time, as well as what type of ICD I might have (there's a standard type that has wires integrated into the heart and is more invasive to fit, requiring more recovery time, or the "subcutaneous" kind that sits in the back of the chest). He also highlighted some questions it would be useful for me to ask.

Once I'd returned from Greece I had a pre-assessment where it was confirmed I would have the subcutaneous ICD.

The Collision Code

It would shock the heart to try to start it again if it stopped, but it wouldn't pace the heart or adjust the rhythm as that wasn't necessary. I had been anxious about it for so long that I was surprised to feel much calmer once a decision had been made and was keen to have it installed as soon as possible.

I called my specialist and said I was ready to go ahead. The procedure happened just before Christmas 2018.

Since then, I've been constantly monitored and, should my heart rhythm change to be outside certain parameters or stop, I will automatically receive a shock to get it back to normal. I have a device next to my bed and every week data is sent to the device clinic at Bart's Hospital who are monitoring me. If it flags anything they will get in touch and let me know if there's something I need to do. There have been three occasions over the years where I've had to go into hospital. It's unbelievable technology and I'm very fortunate to be alive at a time when these things are available. We all are.

While waiting for my operation, I really struggled with my mental health. Being in such limbo with both my heart and with Causr, it was hard to know where I should put my attention. In terms of the business, I made a decision that if I didn't make any progress before the operation, I would close Causr down before going into surgery.

I was seeing a therapist at this time. For years my standard mode of operation had been working all hours of the day cooking up grand visions and plans, but I was failing to do anything close to that. My therapist suggested I try living more in the moment and what I could do on a day-to-day basis. One thing that really centres me is cooking.

Since I'd been taught how to cook properly some years earlier, I've found it a really mindful activity and love the achievement of seeing a meal come together. More so, when it's for other people. Given I had a lot of time on my hands, I decided to host some meals at my home on a BYOB basis with a small contribution to cover costs. Being Jewish, and connected with the London Jewish gay community in particular, I thought that a traditional "Friday night dinner" of soup, roast chicken and vegetables and apple crumble might appeal. I put the word out on a local group and had fourteen people book themselves in.

Food ordered and delivered, I spent the whole day lost in preparations. It was great.

I was reminded of the Onetable dinner I attended with Christine in San Francisco the previous year. I reached out to her and she shared with me the questions she'd used to help get the conversation going. I printed them and turned them into physical cards and, after the first course, invited everyone to take a card from the pack.

The Collision Code

Here are a selection of questions from the deck:

- What ambition are you most embarrassed about?
- What's the one thing you regret not doing?
- What, if anything, is too serious to be joked about?
- For what in your life do you feel most grateful?
- What would constitute a perfect day for you?
- Tell the story behind one of your scars/tattoos.
- Is there something that you've dreamt of doing for a long time? Why haven't you done it?

People were apprehensive at first as they didn't really know each other, but it helped stimulate conversation and really kicked the evening up a gear. I'm not normally one for "organised fun" but this worked really well. In the end people stayed until past midnight, only leaving to get the last trains home.

Feedback afterwards was really positive, and it was the first thing I'd done in a while that had truly distracted me from everything else going on. But I share this story mainly to highlight the value of digging below the surface. This is, of course, another example of how you can create collisions in a fun, relaxed atmosphere. But the questions asked drew us beyond the surface conversations of weather and work and recent activities to find answers that brought people to life. As much as it's great just to find more opportunities to talk to more people, it's even better to grab that opportunity and find a way to go deeper.

Recently, I've evolved this concept of bringing people together into something called "Bagels & Bubbles" where guests bring a bottle or some food to share. I host it at my flat once every quarter, and it's been a fantastic way to connect like-minded people. It's casual, simple, and my friends love it. The relaxed atmosphere makes it easy for everyone to start conversations, and by attending, they feel more confident about engaging with new faces at future events. Plus, in the lead-up to the event, it gives people a perfect excuse and context for people attending to invite new acquaintances, expanding the circle even more naturally.

Reflective Time: How can you create opportunities for deeper connections with others in your life, and what steps might you take to move beyond surface-level conversations?

Goodbye, Causr

Starting is hard. Stopping can be even harder.

I'm not the first person to start something that didn't work out, and I won't be the last. For whatever reason, Causr just wasn't something the world was looking for, or maybe ready for. At any rate, it wasn't wanted.

One notable success we had with Causr was a user who made a £500,000 business deal with a connection he made on the app. When I heard about that I was absolutely elated. It was a huge buzz, and I messaged everyone involved from the team to the investors. At the time it felt like it could be a turning point.

In the end we had over 3,000 users but people weren't staying beyond their initial curiosity and we never got a foothold with any particular group. And despite some positive press coverage, and thousands of emails, phone calls and meetings positioning Causr with schools, alumni networks, corporates, the travel industry and co-working spaces, the positive feedback from people just wasn't enough. I hired dedicated people to work on marketing and partnerships but still we couldn't get the twist of fate we needed for it to take off.

The reality was people liked the idea enough, it just wasn't a priority. At one point I met with one of the world's biggest consultancy firms which was booking over one million hotel nights each year for employees. This felt like an opportunity. With so many people travelling and finding themselves in new places, what connections were being missed internally, let alone externally? I spoke to the innovation team, the travel bookers, procurement, HR and others, and all acknowledged some potential or opportunity to do something. Some even said they were actively discussing ways in which they could help their people connect more and that Causr kept coming up. But it never got any further.

When I started my entrepreneurial journey, there were two people whose paths I crossed time and time again, Thomas and Penny Power. They were the founders of Ecademy, the world's premier social network for small-business people with 650,000 members, starting back in February 1998. The two of them have been a big part of the community and are always helping small businesses and entrepreneurs. Back in 2006, along with Andy Coote, they published *A Friend in Every City: One Global Family—A Networking Vision for the Twenty-First Century*. That meant that when I was working on Causr a meeting with Thomas was all the more meaningful. We met and spoke a number of times about developing Causr for one of the clients Thomas was working with at the time. Once again unfortunately it simply didn't land and progress in a meaningful way that meant nothing was pursued or implemented.

Another firm met with me several times as they said they were interested in a licensing deal worth £50,000 a year for three years with a view to white labelling the service. As a company that spent one billion dollars on travel each year, it seemed a perfect fit (and good value for them!). We got as far as receiving the procurement security criteria but we were barely able to qualify for ten percent of what was needed. This didn't surprise me given our stage and size, but it was a reality check. Conversations continued, but they too petered out.

You do everything you can, and then you do a bit more. But at some point you have to accept the reality.

Those weeks and months that followed were hard, especially with the uncertainty around my heart. I'd kept my investors updated throughout, of course, but I was finding it increasingly hard to summon the energy and belief that was needed to keep going. I didn't have the fight in me to keep pushing Causr to the world. The frustration of rejection after rejection was wearing me down.

A friend of mine, Transformational & Spiritual Teacher, Ryan Mathie, got in touch and we arranged a catch-up in the Shard overlooking London. Over the course of a few hours we talked and he asked me a number of questions to try to help get to the heart of how I was feeling. A topic we kept coming back to was "creating space". It's only when space is created that we can move into it and make things happen. We also talked about slowing down, to speed up. This really resonated with me. Ryan asked me how I thought I'd create some space, and I knew immediately.

Within forty-eight hours I'd booked a flight to Miami for some winter sun. It was exactly what I needed and the first time I really felt better within myself since my diagnosis.

As the summer of 2018 wound on, I kept trying to explore various options for handing Causr over to someone else. I was hoping we could sell what we'd developed, or at least find an elegant way to shut it down. I contacted everyone I'd spoken to along the way, and even offered a completely exclusive licence to the consultancy as a way of giving them the company, without having to go through all the due diligence normally associated with that kind of acquisition.

I didn't get any noes. But I didn't get the yeses I needed. Eventually the time came to close down Causr officially. I started the process of winding things down and and returned what I could and what was left of the investors' money back to the investors. I felt I'd done everything I could do at that stage. I'd even reached out to our main competitor to suggest an acqui-hire situation where I'd work with them. I was pleased I'd given myself permission to have the conversation, but they were too focused on growing their own offering and didn't want to explore anything.

I tried.

Emotionally it was very draining. What if I did just one more call? What if redemption was just around the corner? It might need just one more meeting, one more collision... But I just couldn't go any further down the road.

In December 2018 I officially closed down Causr and so it is no more. In the form of an app at least. As you know from this book the thinking behind it is very much something I'm still keen to pursue.

So why didn't it work?

Was it me? The team? Lack of a real technical co-founder? Not enough money? The expectations of the market? The technology and solution we built? Features we did or didn't include?

There's a quote that seems apt here (often attributed to Winston Churchill), "The difference between success and failure is the ones who fail are the ones that stopped. Those that succeed kept on going." I couldn't go on.

My heart simply wasn't in it anymore.

There's a TED talk that suggests the biggest reason start-ups succeed is timing. Perhaps we were too late. Or maybe too early. Time will tell. I still believe that more communication, community and collaboration are needed in this world.

I'm so grateful to my investors and advisors Simon Franks, Robin Alvarez, Brett Akker and Alex Singer for trusting in me and believing in the idea behind Causr and what I was trying to do. It's people like them who support innovation and drive change that enables us as a society to evolve. Whilst this time Causr didn't work as I've mentioned I hope this book goes some way towards the legacy behind what we were trying to do.

* * *

We live life with a kind of certainty, but more and more I wonder if that's justified. Really, it's a false sense of security, albeit a necessary one, because none of us really know what's around the corner.

Would I still, for example, have left Student Beans to explore Causr if I knew what I now know about my heart? I think I would. Not least, because even if not at that exact moment, the ideas and motivation behind everything I wanted Causr to be have not faded. I would have eventually become frustrated and found myself in need of another outlet.

It is no mystery that everybody dies. But not everybody lives. In hindsight, I think Causr was me trying to really live. And I've not given up on that. But before I tell you the most recent chapter of my story, I want to share what I'd do differently if I had this time again.

If you're working on a project, here are some things I would do:

1. Test the concept better before investing so much time and money.
2. Spend more time with a simple version of the concept before committing time and money to a more complex build.
3. Have a technical co-founder on board and fully committed.
4. Consider how to monetise from the very beginning. With Student Beans we started charging clients be-

fore we'd even launched. With Causr, we had ideas for premium features, but they were never built so we were always playing catch-up.

5. Get paying clients to commit before launch, whether that was by simply getting commitments in writing to promote the tool, or actually inviting clients to pay for the development of the features they really want.

6. Set clearer deadlines for myself and others, and move on if those deadlines are not met. I went back to the same people over and over, and it would have helped a lot to just get a no rather than keep things stringing on.

Mike Butcher (BlueSky/Threads: @mikebutcher)

> Hi James, I hope you are ok!? Just watched your video!

Apr 16, 2021, 10:28 AM

> Anyway, I'm interested in how people network post-pandemic and was reminded of your Causr app. I was wondering if you think it might be more likely to succeed now, given real-world events won't be back for a while

Apr 16, 2021, 10:30 AM

> Do you think people are more open to using location-based apps, especially post-COVID? Or will they be too health conscious about meeting strangers?

Apr 16, 2021, 10:43 AM

It's easy to believe that confidence comes from racking up successes. But it's just as easily generated by learning from failures. If you look at everything as happening *for* you, rather than *to* you then there's something to gain from even the most dire situation.

Still to this day when Causr comes up in conversation as I share about my journey and career the response from most people is that it is/was a good idea. Mike Butcher MBE Editor-at-Large at TechCrunch reached out after Covid in 2021 asking if Causr was more likely to succeed at that time.

I am sure there is a technical solution here still to be explored. Maybe we need to wait for advancements in augmented reality, screens on contact lenses or chips in our brains that mean we know who's nearby and who's "worth" connecting with. In the meantime I believe focusing on what we can do with a little help from *The Collision Code* will enable connections that would otherwise be missed.

Reflection Time: Take a look back at the things that you feel were failures. What have you learnt?

Fully Connected

Whilst I was working on Causr it was an opportunity and excuse to connect with anyone who was passionate about communities and networking often referred to as connectors. One of these very special people was Julia Hobsbawm OBE, an award-winning thought leader who is at the forefront of predicting and advising on the future of work. In June 2017 she published the book *Fully Connected: Surviving and Thriving in an Age of Overload,* which explores a number of related themes. Firstly, we're all more connected than ever, thanks to emails, Facebook, Twitter, Instagram and LinkedIn. However, secondly, we can get overloaded if we end up tweeting, Snapchatting, WhatsApping, obsessing about our inbox twenty-four-seven; ultimately we should take a regular break from social media and invest in some good old-fashioned face-to-face time as well. This is the route to "social health" and wellbeing. Very much the theme, value and importance of *The Collision Code.* After connecting with her she kindly invited me to an event called Networking Nations in Berlin as an attendee with an opportunity to contribute in discussions in August 2017. She also shared Causr with her community contributing to the slowing growing network.

Over the years, to stay connected with people once we've met, my default is to add them on LinkedIn and at various times to keep my connections updated with my latest thinking and ventures I would share a newsletter. Julia was on this list and in June 2019, over two years after we met, she kindly forwarded the update to Derek Draper, the political lobbyist turned psychotherapist and author of *Create Space: How to Manage Time and Find Focus, Productivity and Success.* He reached out and we had a great connection. I read his book and we were exploring ways we could collaborate and work together. Before we got the opportunity to do that he got Covid and weren't in touch again. Derek sadly passed away after he had been critically ill following a cardiac arrest in early December 2023 which, because of the damage inflicted by Covid in March 2020, had led to further complications. Another reminder, if we needed one, of the uncertainty of life, the importance of living in the now and making the most of the time we have.

Are You Enough?

One of the emails I sent to my network was when Causr closed down. I received a short and direct email from John Davy simply saying, "Let's set up a call." John is an amazing person and the connection with him was initially on my eighteenth birthday which I celebrated at Jongleurs Comedy, the company he helped grow into a household name. He signed up to be one of the first users on Causr. When he saw I closed it down and mentioned my coaching practice he introduced me to his wife's Rapid Transformational Coaching course that they were looking for people to provide feedback on.

His wife is Marisa Peer, someone who I also had come across before but hadn't originally made the connection to John. She is a globally acclaimed therapist, best-selling author and award-winning speaker. She also does rapid transformational therapy (RTT®) as well as starting the "I Am Enough" movement. I'm mentioning this here specifically because one of the elements of The Collision Code, as you've read, is confidence. The intention behind each of the stories I've shared is in part to give you the confidence to go out and try things yourself. So often we stop ourselves from being able to achieve or even start or do something because of the lack of belief in ourselves and ultimately thinking we aren't enough. Just remember, according to science, the probability of being born is 400-trillion-to-one, you are a gift and there is no one else like you living your life. If you Google "Marisa Peer I Am Enough" there's lots of videos and content out there and you can read her book. She also has a number of amazing free self-hypnosis sessions I've done that may also be of interest.

What I love about Marisa's approach is the simplicity and the idea that it's rapid and can make a real difference to people. Having worked with one of the people she's trained I can vouch she's the real deal. Whilst different forms of therapy can be useful, I'm not taking anything away from the longer process and weekly sessions. The concept of rapid transform is possible and real and Marisa has made a difference for many thousands of people over the last thirty years. I'm so grateful to have experienced her work and been able to contribute to the launch of her Rapid Transformational Coaching programme.

Reflection Time: Remember this all came about through sending an email to my connections. How are you main-

taining your relationships and keeping in touch with your network?

Coaching

With Causr closed down, and the prospect of a heart transplant hanging over me, I struggled with the idea of planning anything much at all. Every six months I'd have a review to see if I needed to be put onto the list. That in itself has made any hard commitments tricky. Though there's also been a freeing quality to it. It's really helped me prioritise.

Through talking with my therapist, I've realised that I don't really need to worry so much about the long term. This has given me permission to think more deeply about the here and now, and to determine what's possible day to day. It sounds simple, but I realised all I really wanted was to be happy and to contribute something meaningful to the world. If I could do those things while making a living, then I'd be doing great.

Over the years I've always given lots of talks. Some at schools or universities, lots at businesses. After one talk I gave at the University of Birmingham someone called David got in touch to ask for advice on the business he was now running. We met in a local cafe and had a general chat. David left with a list of actions he thought he should take.

Having worked in the entrepreneurial space for many years now, I have gathered so much knowledge and experience.

Sometimes you don't even really realise what you've picked up. In fact, it's often only by speaking to others that you realise there's quite a gap between what you have come to know about a specialist subject, and what others do. I've seen this as another benefit of connecting and making more collisions. After speaking with David in particular, I wondered whether I should be doing more with my knowledge, and even charging for this advice.

I reflected back on my university dissertation "Coaching and the Impact of Coaching on Organisations" and I realised that maybe the answer was staring me in the face all along. It's funny how things come full circle. That said, I was still fighting a whole number of demons related to my heart transplant and I therefore didn't want to overcommit to something I couldn't deliver because, ultimately, I didn't want to let people down.

A few days later I found myself in a shopping centre and spotted a pop-up massage service. The offer was "pay what you like", i.e. what you feel it was worth. It's a concept that's used in a number of places from comedy shows to software, so it seems to work. And I immediately wondered if it could be applied to coaching. It felt less intimidating for me and a potential client, and it felt like the level of commitment I could be comfortable with.

Generally coaches provide specific packages and programmes that run for a number of weeks or months, but

I wanted to provide something that was totally flexible and could adjust to what people actually needed. This seemed especially important for people who hadn't had a coach before who might have no idea whether they needed six weeks or three years.

And so, the concept of "pay-as-you-value" coaching evolved in my mind. I set up a simple registration link on LinkedIn leading to a Google Form. If someone filled it in I would contact them to offer a free discovery call in order to test the fit between us, answer any questions and give a flavour of how I approach coaching. After the discovery call we would set up an initial sixty-minute session at the end of which clients would decide what to pay. That was it.

Family and friends were sceptical about whether it would work. What would happen if people paid less than I was happy with? What if they didn't pay at all? I figured if there was value shared, then it would work itself out. And at the very least, it was worth a try. If it failed, I'd just learn something useful.

I went back to David to tell him what I was doing and positioned myself as a work/life coach and mentor. He said he was keen to talk more and became my first client. We've talked every week since December 2018 with a few breaks for holidays and more recently we've moved to monthly sessions. For the first few months it was just him as a client.

Something I hadn't realised was how freeing it would be to share openly about my heart condition. Given the set-up, I had to be clear that my health might impact our work. We agreed we'd book sessions in the diary but if I couldn't make them he was able to be flexible. It was a weight off my mind that people understood, and it felt good to just be honest. Too often we second guess what others want us to say or do, and often we don't even get it right.

After my ICD operation I was back on calls within two weeks. Because David and I both had work and travel commitments we ran some of our sessions online. Little did we know in 2018 that post-2020 this would very much be the norm.

As I recovered and travelled more to see my partner (who was living overseas) it was also so freeing to take the work with me. I could speak to David from Miami, the Netherlands, Singapore and anywhere else there was an internet connection. It was small compared to my previous business ventures, but it felt right. It was very much me and for David it really worked. Having the space to take that step back and ensure he was focused on the right things, the accountability that someone who leaves a job to become a solopreneur loses, and the support for when things were tough led to a transition from conversations starting with "Will this business succeed?" to "I've just achieved a profit of x this year and I'd like to figure out how many people to hire next year."

Why Do People Have a Coach?

Having spent thousands of hours working with clients, I've gained valuable insights into the coaching process. I've identified three key pillars that illustrate why people choose to work with me, and I believe these principles reflect the broader benefits of coaching. These pillars—space, accountability and support—represent the most common needs expressed by my clients.

S – Space: In our busy lives, we rarely create the space to step back and reflect. Coaching provides that much-needed space. Just like the relief of knowing a holiday is booked, clients feel a sense of ease knowing their session is coming. Even if they struggle to create this space on their own, the coaching session ensures they have dedicated time to pause and reflect.

A – Accountability: There's power in sharing goals with someone else—it adds responsibility. At the end of each session, I ask clients what they want to achieve by the next meeting and how committed they are. This accountability helps them take action, and if they don't, we explore what held them back. Sometimes, the realisation is that their priorities have shifted, which can be as valuable as reaching the original goal.

S – Support: My goal is to see clients succeed, whatever success means to them. Unlike friends and family, who may worry about risks, a coach offers objective support. Whether celebrating wins or navigating challenges, I provide a space for encouragement and reflection. Through questions like "What did you learn?" or "What would you do differently?" clients can reframe setbacks and find new paths forward.

In 2021 I decided to up-skill myself and complete an ACC ICF accredited programme with Optimus Academy, helping me build on my foundations and support my existing and new clients even further. You can read more about this in my chapter I wrote for *The Power of Coaching* published by Optimus Alumni in March 2024: https://bit.ly/thepowerofcoaching

Reflection Time: In what areas of your life could you benefit from creating dedicated space for reflection, accountability and support, and how might you take the first step toward seeking that out?

Jim & Grace

In January 2019 I was still in recovery from my operation when I got a phone call from Enterprise Nation inviting me to speak at the University of Birmingham Student Enterprise launch. They wanted to promote the idea of "student enterprise" and they thought of me. I thought it would be a nice distraction from the aftermath of surgery so I agreed, and booked the train up to Birmingham.

I was met at the station by a student who walked me to the venue. I asked what she was studying and she told me she was doing a biomedical science degree looking at how different medications (including heart medications) affect the body. I mentioned briefly about my condition, but she was preoccupied and didn't really seem to notice the coincidence.

The evening and my talk went well. I hadn't spoken publicly about my health condition as it wasn't really part of the story, but my feeling in general was if it comes up, it comes up. I certainly don't want to hide it or suggest I'm embarrassed by it. At the end of the session the audience was invited to ask questions and the host and founder of Enterprise Nation, Emma Jones, responded initially by asking me, "What's next for you?" (I'd ended my talk by noting the closure of Causr.)

I paused and reflected. Then I swallowed.

"I've just been diagnosed with hypertrophic cardiomyopathy," I said, and went to explain the details and my recent surgery. It was hard to articulate it all and I could feel myself getting emotional. As I spoke I noticed the room had gone completely silent. And then, I finished. The room burst into applause, I smiled appreciatively, and I sunk back into my seat to listen to the other speakers.

After the event was over, a student at the university, Grace Lynskey, approached me to thank me for sharing my story. She told me about her twin brother, Jim, who'd been born with viral meningitis which damaged his heart and has significantly impacted his health over the years. She said he'd been on and off the transplant list most of his life and gave me her details so she could connect us.

Grace and Jim set up Save9Lives, a campaign which promotes the simple message that one person can save, or enhance, the lives of nine others through organ donation. When I spoke to Jim, it was inspiring to hear about his experience of living with heart failure. His specific condition was called dilated cardiomyopathy and it had caused his heart to become weakened and enlarged. In 2015, his heart had reached chronic failure and he began his wait for a donor. Knowing that he was just one of 6,000 sons, daughters, mothers and fathers on the transplant list he founded Save9Lives to try to do something to give him and his family a better chance.

A few days after we spoke, a card arrived in the post.

Dear James,

I hope this finds you well! Just a note to say thank you for sharing your experiences recently. I know it may be a little overwhelming at times to adjust to your defib, but know you always have an ear here if you need support :-)

Thank you for the initial chat about Save9Lives too—it means a lot!

All my best,

Jim

Part III Moving Forward

Dear James,

I hope this finds you well! Just a note to say thank you for sharing your experiences recently. I know it may be a little overwhelming at times to adjust to your defib, but know you always have an ear here if you need support ☺ Thank you for the initial chat about Save9Lives too - it means alot! All my best,

Jim

I only spoke to Jim a couple of times, but he was a fine young man; brave, strong and resilient. The generosity and selflessness of his actions are a true testament to his character.

On 13 May 2019, Jim died. He was just twenty-three years old.

I'm still in touch with Grace, and so grateful that Emma asked that question which led to these wonderful collisions. And I am grateful too that I chose to open up, be authentic and vulnerable. Perhaps it's what we're most afraid of sharing that is sometimes the key to a real connection. It would have been very easy to give an empty, waffly answer. But because I didn't, I met someone very special indeed who made me feel less alone. Thank you, Jim.

Reflection Time: When have you chosen to be vulnerable or share something personal, and how did that openness impact the connections or relationships you formed as a result?

Time for Change

As you have probably picked up by now, I love to travel. And so not being able to has been particularly hard to comprehend. Since my diagnosis, partly with this in mind, I have always questioned my doctors and others as to how far I can push myself and what I can safely do. At various stages I've had push back from those responsible for my health, but

Part III Moving Forward

I've reasoned that as long as I have suitable insurance and can feel the life left in me, I know what I can do. And I want to *live*. And so, in March 2019, after my operation, I was planning to travel to Asia.

At the time, my father was working in Singapore, so my partner Michael and I flew out with him on one of his trips. Singapore itself was generally rainy, hot and humid—not great at all for my condition—but we were only there a few days and I enjoyed it. We spent our last night in the amazing Marina Bay Sands Hotel and spent time in the world's highest infinity pool. You can't do that in Kentish Town!

Next we travelled to Hong Kong, then Macau and from there onto Beijing to prepare for the highlight of the trip: a visit to the Great Wall of China.

Michael had found an amazing tour guide who somehow knew exactly where to go, and when, so that nobody else was around. We were part of a small tour party of six, and they hiked up to the wall section while I took a leisurely gondola ride with not another person in sight. I arrived at the top to the most serene surroundings with rolling hills as far as I could see.

I spent about an hour deep in thought about where I had come from to get to this moment. All the things I'd done, the stuff that had worked and that hadn't, the challenges I'd faced and my newly embraced heart condition. Then

I looked out across the landscape and tried to look into my future.

James on top of The Great Wall of China

I didn't get any answers, but I did know I needed more structure than I'd been giving myself. I had been working with David on coaching calls during the trip but it wasn't something I felt I could keep doing in such an ad hoc way.

As the others arrived, we stayed on the wall until sunset. It was beautiful. And as the daylight faded, I could feel its warmth and light transferring itself to the next phase of my life.

I was ready to go home and let it begin.

Reflection Time: Have you ever had a moment during a trip or after a big life event where you paused to think about your future? What did you learn about where you want to go next?

A Plan

When I returned from China I had a very clear idea about what I wanted to do:

- Get up every day and be happy
- Have at least one client a day Monday to Friday

That way I could go to sleep every single night knowing I'd made a difference, and on my own terms. And as long as I could generate the right revenue per client (which was all down to how well I gave them something to value), then I had every box ticked.

With this in motion, I realised I was living a very intentional life. I had a clear purpose (to help someone each day) and everything could just be built to serve that. There was such clarity for me in giving myself permission to live like this.

I did, however, need some more clients. So I shared widely within my network that I was looking to take on more people for coaching and posted in some online startup groups. Within three months I'd hit my target and I've been consistently on target every month since.

Consistency, in fact, has been a key part of what's helped me to keep going. In October 2020 I was really struggling to breathe and starting to seriously worry. I had my second heart transplant assessment on the horizon and everything was feeling very heavy. Yet I continued to work with clients, even if that meant getting up, getting dressed, delivering a session and falling straight back into bed. I still haven't cancelled one session due to my condition, and I'm incredibly proud of that. Of course I've structured things to make that possible, but I really feel that it's my clients who help me as much as I help them. As you'll know from reading this book, I really need to be around people, having conversations and making those collisions—no matter how tiny—to energise me and drive me through life. This is a way I can continue to have that whatever the circumstances.

Going further, I wanted to use this new way of working to realise a long-held ambition to spend the summers somewhere warm, and the winters skiing. I suppose without my heart condition I might have eventually had the success required to retire early enough to try that out. As it happens, I've been forced into it and living my dream at thirty-six.

Let me rewind. In 2019 I found a place to rent in Morzine, France. It's a beautiful resort nestled in the Alps with great skiing and a lovely community. Given I was used to travelling so much and with a partner living overseas, I really had no need to be stuck in London. There was nothing to keep me pinned down, and it was certainly never relaxing.

And so, I took the leap. I now spend my time between France, and travelling all over the world. When I need to, I simply head to London for doctor's visits and to spend time with my family. With a cardiologist assessment every six months I know that I have those to build my year around now, and when I'm told things are OK and that I can come back in six months it's the best gift anyone could ask for. A literal new lease of life. For now, at least, I'm embracing it and building on everything I've ever collided with to live with intention, reflecting on what's right for me and harnessing my knowledge and experience to make that happen.

You might be thinking, "OK, James, but we can't all do that." And, of course, that's true. While I have serious issues to contend with, I am in the privileged position that I have my business experience to fall back on. But that wasn't always the case. By accident or design I am now reaping the rewards of a lifetime of collisions. I'm just doing it sooner than I thought possible.

Why did I have to become so ill to make it happen? Why do people generally need such a shock to the system to redirect their lives? There are many sensible answers to that I suppose, but I only care about what it will take for *you*. What will it take for you to start living?

I can't blame you if you don't know the answer. I didn't, until I did. And I don't wish heart complications on anyone. But somehow, in the midst of everything, in what could have been the darkest time of my life, I've found myself utterly focused on being who I want to be.

And, of course, I'm finding new ways to make more collisions...

Reflection Time: What would living with more intention look like for you, and what small steps could you take today to start moving in that direction?

Morzine

When I moved to Morzine I wanted to do something within the community that would make a difference. There are three initiatives that I came up with, and each has thrived in its own way.

Chairlift Chats

Earlier, I suggested meeting people on chairlifts as a great way to connect with people. You have a limited amount of time, which minimises the potential for awkwardness, and it's an easy context to get chatting about your holiday, or work, in the resort. Combining my passions for skiing and as a coach I had the idea to further support the community by offering "Chairlift Chats" where we would meet for a ski, have some coaching whilst on the chairlift and then continue with our skiing. It's something I offer to the community each season and it's amazingly powerful as it gives people a set time to explore an idea or concept and then, whilst skiing, find the time and focus to process their thoughts properly and move forward. What passions could you combine?

Morzinebylocals.com

When I arrived, there was a 40,000-strong Facebook group called 'Morzine Crew!'. Every day, people were asking the same questions and getting the same answers, so I had the idea of putting together a simple spreadsheet that covered the most common topics: which transfer company to use, good restaurants and so on. Doing so took me back to the work on needanumber.co.uk so many years ago. Since launching, the spreadsheet has been viewed almost 11,000 times. Whilst people keep telling me I could turn this kind of support into a business, it's been such a great way of supporting the community, giving back. And it's given me more context to connect and speak with anyone.

Morzine Solos & Friends

As you've read, I've long experimented with community projects such as Shareatable, FriendlyFriday, Causr and Kentish Cluster. So it will come as no surprise that I wanted to see what I could do up in the mountains.

I searched online for anything already going but couldn't find anything and so, the Facebook group "Morzine Solo Travellers & Friends" was launched in September 2019 in the run-up to the 2019/20 ski season. I initially invited a few people I knew and slowly the numbers ticked up. Various people posted and connected with each other. The season that never was (2020/21) came and went, then 2021/22 started. As COVID-19 was still an issue it was a slightly disjointed season that winter and I used the group to host a couple of ski meet-ups to make things a bit more cohesive.

A member of the group messaged me after his three-week trip to thank me for starting the group. He shared that in the whole time he'd been in Morzine he hadn't had to snowboard alone once by connecting with people he'd met in the group. He created a video to share online about his holiday and gave a thank you credit to me. I was thrilled. By the time summer rolled around we also organised some walks in the mountains, and by the time winter 2021/22 rolled around, there were 300 people in the group.

That winter started with some pretty terrible weather for skiing. It rained for ten days straight, while on 1 January it was fourteen degrees. They opened the lifts for mountain biking, and the tennis courts were still in use. But as the weather turned colder and the snow returned, the person who had made the video the year before messaged me to invite me for a drink. On the same day someone called Scott messaged me too about meeting and so I invited them both to have a mid-week drink. But as I thought about it, I thought there was no reason not to open the invite further. I checked with them both, and together we put it out to the whole group. Almost twenty people turned up on a Wednesday night and so began a tradition, somewhat by accident, of "Mid-Week Drinks", often in a different venue, always welcome to all. It's amazing to think that instead of coming together, we could all be sitting in the same bar or pub alone not speaking to each other.

Morzine Solos & Friends also gave me the permission, context and confidence to go and meet the local community and venues. This helped me build relationships as well as practising my French—another great example of creating something for the community that enabled me to create many more collisions for myself. I'm now very much part of the community and can barely leave the apartment without saying hello (or *bonjour!*) to someone I know.

The first week hosting drinks I thought everyone seemed to find me easily enough, but someone ended up posting on Facebook, "It's all well and good organising drinks, but what's the point if we can't find you!!" It's a fair point, and it prompted me to contact a ski clothing company called OOSC to ask if they wanted me to do some promotion in return for some ski wear that would help people identify me and the group. They agreed and sent me a bright rainbow-coloured ski suit. It was a nice example of a pseudo-commercial deal being done for the benefit of the community. Nothing complex, nothing to negotiate over, just a simple win–win for everyone. And in terms of starting that conversation, the context of the meet-ups made it easy for me to ask, and much easier than if I was doing it for my own means.

On one occasion I was stopped by a group member while out in my rainbow OOSC suit on the slopes. We chatted for a bit before he turned to his young son and said, "James is doing something really important for the community—he's helping people make friends." I'd never thought of it in that way, but it really resonated.

Each week, during the season, one of the group members Nigel hosted a quiz team at a local quiz night and there are also many weekly ski meet-ups. In hindsight, which is maybe obvious, the weekly drinks meet-ups were a real catalyst that enabled people to meet and make connections. It's much more casual and easy to attend than meeting on a ski slope, for example. But having even the slightest connection through Facebook, then in a bar, and then on the slopes was an easy progression for people. It was fun to see it in action.

Over the season we saw people join the group who were in town for just a few days, or working there the whole season, or even living locally. It was a real split of ages and men and women and people from all over the world. And the feedback was great. For something so simple, it seemed to generate a lot of value for people. Someone told me they specifically came to Morzine because of the group. Others mentioned they have been for years but not really met many people. That had all changed thanks to the group. As it gained this popularity and operated year round, we simplified the name to "Morzine Solo & Friends".

People often thank me for what I do and the community I've created but I always reply and thank them for turning up, if they didn't it would just be me sitting by myself!. A big thank you to Jenny, Liz, Nigel, Hannah, Gráinne, Ben, Rhiannon, Stephen, Morag, Kathy & Stephen, Jon and the

Johns (at last count there were four!) Nathan, Lorna, Tommy & Tom and the many others who show up, contribute and remain part of the community.

Maria was also a core part of the 2022/23 season from hosting a flame-lit walk around the lake to drinking mulled wine after climbing up a tree and many more things. She continued the trend after leaving Morzine and has helped establish the Crans Montana Solos & Friends Community.

While it may seem simple, I hope you'll also recognise the power of a group like this to create collisions. Moreover, I hope you'll see that this is something you can do, and that you should! The group in Morzine gives people context, permission and confidence to make the most of their time in the mountains, be that long or short. It provides a platform for events that offer the same, and it acts as glue that takes a host of disparate individuals and makes them feel part of something communal. It's very social, it's very human and it's such, such fun. February 2025 there are now over 4,500 members and the number continues to grow every day.

I love to watch as people join the group as strangers and slowly transition through their first event, to being a core part of the group that year, or beyond. And I can't possibly know how many interesting things have emerged from collisions between group members, but I know the world and resort would be less rich without it, and groups like it.

All I did was register the name and start something small; it's the community that picks it up and makes it special. Everything I've shared, everything I've told you, is simply about setting the ball rolling.

As I said at the beginning, it might help to think of yourself like a ball on a snooker table. You can roll along smoothly for as long as there's space ahead of you, and that's OK. But when you come across another ball you have the chance to benefit from a collision, taking off on a trajectory that's new and interesting and could take you anywhere.

I think that's exciting. I know it's powerful. And I hope you agree with me that it's what makes life worth living.

It can be as simple as starting or joining a Facebook group, introducing yourself to someone new, or meeting up with someone who reaches out to you. It's as easy as attending an event instead of staying home or saying hello instead of staying silent. These are small actions you can take any day, no matter where you are or what you're doing. You just need a bit of a plan, and I hope that the Code (permission, confidence and context) will help guide your way.

Connecting the Dots: Embracing Life

I'm greatly inspired by a quote from the commencement speech that Steve Jobs gave at Stanford in 2005.

"You can't connect the dots looking forward; you can only connect them looking backward. So you have to trust that the dots will somehow connect in your future. You have to trust in something—your gut, destiny, life, karma, whatever. This approach has never let me down, and it has made all the difference in my life."

As I've recalled the stories in this book, I've thought of each of them as a dot. One of them relayed the story of sitting next to Muhammed Yunus. "Trust," he said. "Trust you are doing the right thing, you are where you are meant to be, doing what you are meant to be doing."

In October 2020 whilst the world was grappling with Covid I managed to get an infection on my foot whilst stepping on something in the sea in Greece. Instead of going straight to the doctor I went to the pharmacy and got some cream for it. It got progressively worse over the coming days and put me on crutches. I flew home early and had to change the bandage myself over the next couple of weeks with video support from a nurse. Thanks to Covid, and the fact that I'd been travelling, I couldn't see anyone face to face. Shortly after my return to London my Apple watch alerted me to a change in my heart rhythm. It was racing and I was feeling really uneasy. I contacted my specialist in Bart's in London and the team at Papworth and appointments were scheduled for both.

My heart rate was going up to 170 beats per minute whilst I was stationary—something wasn't right. They immediately put me on a drug called bisoprolol which brought my heart rate down and I was told my heart rhythm had changed and I was now experiencing "atrial fibrillation". I was convinced it was connected to the infection on my foot, but the doctors considered it to be an inevitable process and a natural next stage of my condition. This, they said, was always going to happen. I was also put on a drug called amiodarone to help change the rhythm and calm the heart rate down.

Due to the foot infection and being on crutches, the visit to Papworth was delayed as the transplant assessment involves a walking exercise and I was still struggling to stand for any period of time.

Bisoprolol combined with the amiodarone was doing its job and slowing my heart rate down but it meant I couldn't do anything and was really struggling to move. My Apple watch showed a gradual reduction in my resting heart rate from an average of 76 beats per minute (BPM) down to just 51 BPM, but I couldn't get out of bed. It was Saturday morning and I was due to drive to Papworth on Sunday for the assessment on Monday morning. I emailed my specialist updating her on the situation and that I was bedridden. I included the readings from my Apple watch showing the decline over the last few days. (As a side note, whilst the Apple watch isn't a recognised medically approved device, it has helped give me confidence and data to back up what my body is doing and how my heart is behaving/beating. I've found it very useful in that respect for many years now.)

To my surprise and great appreciation she replied within thirty minutes telling me to stop taking the bisoprolol and lower the amiodarone dose. I did what she said and within hours felt better. The following day Michael, my brother, drove me up to Cambridge. When we stopped at the service station I almost collapsed, but we got there. I did the assessment and various tests over the next couple of days with results coming thick and fast.

My ejection fraction had gone from fifty-one percent down to forty-nine percent and my NT-proBNP level was over 14,000. Ejection fraction is a measurement, expressed as a percentage, of how much blood the left ventricle pumps out with each contraction. Normal is between fifty and seventy percent. For the NT-proBNP level, above 100 is not normal. This is the highest it's ever been for me—the protein is produced when the heart is working harder. This wasn't good. My heart was failing and it was the first time I was told it was up to me, but if I chose to go on the transplant list they would support my decision. In my head I blamed the infection, change in rhythm and then the medication for why I was struggling so much now. I made the decision to not go on the list there and then as I'd just stopped the medication and thought I would get better. They were monitoring me and I would see the specialists every three months anyway. At the same time if anything changed and either I didn't get better or I got worse, I could always go back to them.

The Collision Code

On paper it was time for a heart transplant, but I wasn't ready. One of the statistics that always comes back to the front of my mind when making this decision is the average life expectancy after having a heart transplant: eleven years. The Guinness Book of World Records confirmed a Dutch man as the world's longest-surviving heart transplant recipient. Bert Janssen, fifty-seven, has lived with a donor heart for thirty-nine years and counting. Mr Janssen was diagnosed with cardiomyopathy at age seventeen. From everything I understand the aim is to live with my current heart as long as possible. It's also about quality of life. I think, *Are there things I want to do but I can't due to the limitations my health puts on me?*

For around three weeks I lived with my dad as I was healing from the foot infection, I was breathless and bedridden. I struggled to get out of bed, walk up the stairs, let alone walk in the street. If I didn't improve I would go on the list and it would have been time. But I did improve.

I was seeing my specialists every three months, but in December 2021 I remember friends visiting London and still feeling very tired every day. We would go for a walk in the morning then I would go home to rest and join them again in the evening. I had another follow up with Papworth and whilst the readings were better now at fifty-one percent ejection fraction I could still technically go on the list and they would support my decision. Once again I thought, *Is there anything that I want to do that I can't currently do?* Skiing is a big passion of mine, as you know, and I remember flying out to be in France thinking I hadn't skied since March 2020 and if I arrived and I couldn't do it due to my health then it would be time to go on the list. I landed on 17 December just before France prohibited people from the UK entering the country. I skied on 18 December and just remember the sheer joy, happiness and relief that I could still do it and felt great for doing it.

The challenge with the heart transplant is you need to be well enough to have the transplant but not too unwell for it not to take. There's a window of opportunity and then a fine line. I've been told it will take on average between 200 to 300 days to get a transplant in the UK for someone of my age, height, blood type and build. Once you are on the list you need to be within four hours of the hospital and be ready to go at any moment. They have had situations where people have been listed, sent home and that night been called to have the transplant. The challenge is a decision needs to be made knowing where your health might be in 200 to 300 days—over half a year away. When it was suggested I could go on the list I thought I was going to get better, and I did.

But now I feel like I'm walking this fine line. It reminds of the startup world and the fine line between success and failure. Knowing when to give up and walk away and when to keep going.

The Collision Code

The doctors said I was likely to have a transplant within three to five years. We're now in year seven. I know how quickly things can deteriorate and that's the challenge with my condition. It's why I have the defibrillator in, it's why footballers and marathon runners die from my condition because the body overcompensates and lives with the condition, but then the heart eventually can't do enough.

We might never know when the right time to go on this list is until it's too late. The hope is we will make the right call at the right time. I say "we", as for now it's been my decision, my choice, but there's an inevitability that a time will come where it will no longer be my choice but a necessity and the doctors will say it's time. If there are too many days in a row, that I can't breathe, I can't walk, I can't ski or do the things I want to do and the medication can't keep up with the body (my weight increases due to water retention starting with my feet swelling), I'm tired and can't get out of bed like I was in October 2020, it will be time.

It was while waiting for the December appointment that this sense of overwhelm came over me that I've felt a number of times over the years. Something I couldn't shake was the realisation that if something happened to me, these stories and this message would be lost. I had to write the book now and so, here it is. I hope you enjoyed it, I hope it challenges you and I hope it has inspired you to create more connections and collisions.

Once I decided this book needed to happen, I shared with my network I was looking for help and so began the conversations with friends, editors, writers and agents. After an introduction from Rachel Davies to John Monks I was then introduced to Cate Caruth who helped refine the first draft. It was then on 29 June 2023, old friends Matthew Stafford and Katie Lewis were launching their book *Find Your 9others*. 9others is a network where you meet nine others for dinner to share business challenges often starting with the question "What's keeping you up at night?" It was here I asked Matthew how he got the book together. He shared that he had connected with Robbie Dale who I knew from The Marketing Academy—we had already worked together on the FriendlyFriday campaign. Not only that, Matthew and Robbie had originally connected on Causr as one of the first users on the platform. I reconnected with Robbie and over the best part of 2024 he helped refine, write and rewrite, craft and turn my narrative and stories into what it is today. I'm so grateful to him for everything that he's done to help tell this story and make *The Collision Code* a reality.

Too often we wait until something bad or unruly happens to us, or someone we know, for us to remember life is short. Too often we're forced to make a change, yet it's one we know we should have made earlier. Hopefully my story is another example to you that no one knows what's around the corner. Life is short. You have to do what you want to do now.

The Collision Code

On the one hand I would give anything to go back to not knowing there was anything wrong, but the silver lining is I'm living with intention and more balanced than I ever have been. It's one of the reasons why I filmed a YouTube series about my heart health called "Heart Matters: Living with Intention" (https://www.youtube.com/@james_eder/). These are short videos aimed to help people living with a chronic condition, to raise awareness of hypertrophic cardiomyopathy and more broadly to help remind people that no one knows how long we've got.

Let me be the wake-up call so you don't need to wait for your own one.

I was interviewed once and asked a question about work–life balance. I answered in the same way I always do with my belief that work is part of your life, and instead of work–life balance it's really a question of whether you're enjoying it or not. When I was working on both Student Beans and Causr, most of the days didn't feel like work. So that was a great balance for me.

But recently a friend came to visit me in France who runs a business and asked me why I wasn't running another company. I pointed to the view of the mountains and asked him a simple question: "What for?" How much is enough?

My coaching work fulfils me for now. I can help others on their journey and, right now, that's enough. It might change in the future, but for now I keep in mind an exercise I do with my clients that asks the following questions:

- What does your ideal year look like?
- What does your ideal quarter look like?
- What does your ideal month look like?
- What does your ideal day look like?
- What does your ideal weekday look like?
- What does your ideal weekend look like?

As long as the answers match what I'm up to, then it's going OK. It doesn't have to be more complicated than that.

And as I've started to live with intent in this way, I've started to spot ways in which the world might be gradually moving in the right direction.

There are currently many talks and experiments being done around the "four-day work week". I believe that this is one of the shifts that will enable people to have more balance in their lives giving people more time. I've also been about "blue zones", areas of the world where people live longer, better lives. This is a concept Dan Buettner and his team have dedicated research time into, trying to find what these people have in common. What they found was nothing extreme, simply a balance of good health habits and social engagement. Buettner listed nine factors, including: moderate, regular physical activity, life purpose, stress reduc-

The Collision Code

tion, moderate caloric intake, a plant-based diet, moderate alcohol intake, especially wine, engagement in spirituality or religion, engagement in family life, and engagement in social life as the lifestyle habits leading to long, healthy life.

If you've not yet heard of blue zones I'd encourage you to look them up. There's a series on Netflix about them and you can start by looking at bluezones.com. My hope is that this book goes some way to helping people engage more socially, creating the connection we need to make us happier and healthier and play a small part in the movement towards more fulfilling lives.

There's a video that's done the rounds online that invites the viewer to imagine they had a bank account filled with £86,400 at midnight every day. The only catch is that by 11:59 p.m. it would have trickled away if not spent. In that situation, you would spend all of that money, right? Well, each day we *are* given 86,400 of something. Not money, but time: this is the number of seconds we've got each and every day. We can all do more to use those seconds wisely. But the great thing is, if today didn't go the way you wanted or how you thought you wanted it to go, you get the opportunity to start again and decide what you want to be different tomorrow.

I started this final section with a Steve Jobs quote. I'll end it there too. Every morning Steve Jobs would ask himself, "If today were the last day of my life, would I want to do what

I am about to do today? If the answer is 'no' for too many days in a row, I know I need to change something."

Life is too short.

You deserve to be happy.

The world is waiting for you.

You just need to go and collide.

Live using the Code.

The Big Clear Out

Whilst many of you were perfecting the art of banana bread or your home workout routine I chose to take the clear out route during lockdown.

A cuddly toy.... An iMac.... A boomerang.... 150 safety pins... LA Fitness Bag... A blackberry pearl.... 5 wired magazines.... 1x Nokia E61 and the list goes on.... it sounds like something out of the old television programme, The Generation Game with Bruce Forsyth.

Whilst I was away during the first lockdown I had clear out envy and was only too ready when I got back to my home in London, a big declutter was overdue. The big area to clear was the space underneath the stairs where after moving in 7 years ago back in 2014 I put everything I didn't want or need access to behind a closed door and forgot about it. 6 old mobile phones, laptops, old watches & boxes & boxes of....... stuff.

The Collision Code

After my heart rhythm changed I had put the idea of the big clear out on the back burner. I was slowly getting my energy back and being stable again when I watched Minimalism - on Netflix. Having been fortunate to have travelled a lot over the last few years living on barely more than a couple of carry-on bags it made me reflect on why do I really need all this stuff? As the documentary showed, mainstream society has conditioned us that things can make us happy. If I buy this then I'll be happy. It might make us happy in the moment but that soon fades and we want something else but where does it end?

I'm not saying get rid of everything you own. I am saying Do you need everything you have? Do you love everything you have? And do you want everything you have? I'm certainly not there yet and as one person in the programme stated they have catalogued everything they own and it's less than 50 items, I'm a long way off that. My journey of giving & selling continues but I'm also more mindful than ever of what and when I buy. You can't take this stuff with you when you're gone. Whilst it might sound morbid the truth is anything you leave behind someone else is going to have to sort it out so whoever that might be why not give them a head start. I thought I'd share my attempt at my minimalist journey so far below;

Initially I started using OLIO, the foundations started with Food Waste. (Plug: OLIO an app that connects neighbours to share surplus food and other household items, all for free #sharemorewasteless www.olioex.com) Founded by the incredible Tessa Clarke and Saasha Celestial-One some of the most mission led founders I know.

I ordered some quince during an online supermarket order - which to be honest I thought they were a type of pear due to their shape. When they arrived I didn't know what to do with them. While you can make various things like jam or a tart I decided I wasn't inspired so why not give them away on OLIO.

Quince not Pears!

Within thirty minutes I had three requests for the Quince. I selected the person closest to me who was just less than five-hundred meters away and within another thirty minutes the 4 quinces were gone.

Since I started with OLIO I've given away over 40 items the Quince, 4 cushions from IKEA, IKEA cutlery separator, Two New York Yankee nibble / dips novelty bowls, Apple iWatch stand, La fitness gym bag, 2 suit travel covers, Tim tam cooler bag, Queen size inflatable mattress (with a small hole I couldn't find!), Mini bathroom bins, DVD players, Laptop bag, Iphone 7 / 8 case, White table cloth approx 132 cm by 228, Vuvuzela - loud horn, Blue small lamp, Bonsai tree pot and dish and trimming scissors, Weighing scale, A1 flip chart paper approx 25 sheets, Meal planner magnet and pen, Bathroom toothbrush cup, Rat and mouse repeller, White shoe laces, Gap linen record bag, Usb Presentation clicker, Collapsable Laundry basket, Cutlery tray, 3 new promo mugs, Tin of pins, Photo frame, Selection of coloured glitter pots, 3 hats and 3 fun glasses, Inflatable travel pillow with fleece cover in bag, Analog tv aerial, Usb powered scanner, Scanner / printer Epson xp - 247, Multi pocket bag & 100% waterproof rain jacket. The 40 items that went to new homes and not landfill. I have to admit it was slightly addictive and such a joy to know other people are getting to use and enjoy what I was just pleased to get out of my life!

Continuing along the clear out lines to help find things a new home I also gave a few bags of clothes I donated to an Oxfam Clothes Bank.

I also took a number of DVDs and other items in good condition to The British Heart Foundation charity shop.

Part III Moving Forward

In my building I also left a box out of things for people to collect and it all disappeared within a day X 1 Toms sticker x 1 yellow tinted sunglasses X 4 magnetic catches X 1 white face paint X 1 strength ball X 2 soft glass cases and cleaner X 1 travel plug X 1 cap X 2 mobile phone / wallet stickers X 1 luggage tag X 150 safety pins X 1 stress brain ball and x 1 stress buster inflatable! X 2 bottle opener key rings X 2 other key rings X 1 belt, x 1 business card holder x1 mobile phone pop socket. X 1 Eye shade, x 1 micro card adapter and a couple of other things...

Speaking to a close friend who was in support of the clear out and an eBay advocate she suggested giving it a go.

The first item I sold was a wearable sleeping bag. Off to a great start it sold for £60. eBay has an amazing function where you can donate a % to a charity so I choose to donate 10% of anything sold to The British Heart Foundation. It's an amazing function and lets buyers know that part of the sale gets donated.

And the sales continued... LA Fitness Sports towel... Twilight Saga - 4 Film Collection The Story So Far DVD 4-Disc Box-Set..... The Wire - Series 1-5 - Complete (DVD, 2008, 24-Disc Set, Box Set)..... easyblinds Portable Travel Blackout Blind - Extra Large..... Harry potter complete 8 film collection..... The Complete Matrix Trilogy DVD Set... The Beatles Yellow Submarine Playing Cards unused mint unopened.... Vera men's watch W0084.... Joblot Usb Stick Collection Of 42 Approx 55 gb of storage space.... Animal Time To Ride Titanium Watch Model 050...... Gents Sekonda Xpose Watch.... British airways / American Airlines Aeroplane Usb Stick... TOM TOM GO 4V00.710 SatNav with UK maps preloaded memory card.... Handspring Visor PDA Organiser Palm With Leather Case Docking Station And CD.... Apple MB528LL/A iPod Touch 2nd Generation - Black.... Ted Baker Men travel suit bags.... Original Apple iPod Firewire Charger (Firewire to 30-pin).... IBM 1GB Microdrive Media Storage Hard Disc.... Nokia 6630 - 3 UK - Retro Good Condition.... Original MacBook Air Apple MB003B/A MacBook Air A1237 13.3" Laptop... Sekonda Xpose Scuba Mens Quartz Watch With Date Model no. 3015.... Apple Mac Book Air 13 inch, mid-2011, 1.7GHz i5, 4GB RAM, No HD, for parts.... The Original Apple iPad 1st generation 32gb silver *not working* For Parts Only...... Nokia 6288 - 3 Network - Internal Memory Card - Working Condition..... Memorex 3" CD-R 50 Blank CDs 21 Mins 185mb Up To 16x On Spindle With 5 Cd-Rw..... So far the item total is £479.90 the amount after postage and tax. Not a bad start. There's still a few more items to go.

Facebook Market Place: Another friend suggested Facebook Market Place as another good place to sell. Whilst it feels less secure and often people exchange cash I sold a digital camera, neon gaffer tape, Ikea bedside light, a wooden carving, waterproof jacket, a couple of hair clippers, 4 stackable chairs and a number of other things. In total making around £100.

Nextdoor: Another localised listing site is https://nextdoor.co.uk/ - Here I sold a sofa, sandwich toaster, Colombian poncho, Soda Stream Cordial. I also donated a number of pillows and general bedding to a person collecting for the homeless as many of the charity shops don't accept these items.

It's worth listing in multiple places and relatively easy once you've taken the photos and written the description once.

A summary of places I sold / gave things away to:

- OLIO
- The British Heart Foundation
- Oxfam Clothes Bank
- ebay.
- Trash for Nothing
- Freegle
- Facebook Market Place
- Nextdoor

Whilst lockdown involved social distancing drop offs and collections it was still an opportunity to 'meet' likeminded people especially on Olio where the community are super responsive and you can tell are committed to making sure we keep things from landfill. A couple of interesting people stood out from a person who was a body / security guard for an ambassador's family to a lady running a new Gin business.

As I said earlier on I've still got a way to go as the journey continues to have less, being happier and living more.

I feel lighter. It really is a great way of living.

If you're interested in more about how to go about your own clear out take a look at the Introductory Declutter, Clear Out Guide I've put together in the resources section at the end of this book.

Reflection Time: What could you give away? What are you holding on to that you no longer need or no longer serves you?

My Personal Development, Leadership and Health Journey: What's Yours?

Over my life I've been fortunate enough to participate in some amazing leadership and development programmes. I wanted to shine a light on them here to give you a flavour of the lifetime of investment, and the importance of a growth mindset that has helped me over the years. It's been decades of time spent on all areas of my life, from work to relationships and now my health and wellbeing. There's no shortcut, and you'll see the breadth and scale below. But whatever base you're starting from, the best time to get started on your own journey is now.

Books/Audible/Podcasts/YouTube: Starting here as it's probably the most easily accessible area (plus, you're already reading this!). One of the best practices to get into the habit of reading more is to target ten pages or ten minutes a day. Or alternatively, a goal of one book a month. You could also "habit stack" by reading whilst you are commuting, or listening to audiobooks while cleaning.

Here are my top ten books:

1. *The Naked Leader*, **David Taylor:** According to David Taylor—one of Europe's most successful speakers

on leadership and personal development—the most important discovery you can make is to discover who you really are. Everything you need to be, anything you want, you already have; there is no right or wrong, there is only what serves you, and what does not; what you think about, you are, what you focus on, you will become; and if you give yourself permission, you will achieve every dream and every ambition you've ever had. This is one of the books that has impacted me the most.

2. ***The Power of Now* and *A New Earth*, Eckhart Tolle:** In *The Power of Now*, Tolle demonstrates how to live a healthier, happier, mindful life by living in the present moment. Oprah Winfrey said, "I keep Eckhart's book at my bedside. I think it's essential spiritual teaching. It's one of the most valuable books I've ever read." To make the journey, you will need to leave your analytical mind and its false created self, the ego, behind. Although the journey is challenging, Eckhart Tolle offers simple language and a question-and-answer format to show us how to silence your thoughts and create a liberated life. Do you feel unhappy or unfulfilled? Tired and stressed? Lacking focus and energy? Then you need Eckhart Tolle's *A New Earth*. In this ground-breaking classic, he gives you the spiritual framework to: understand yourself better, manage, manifest and achieve your goals,

reach your full potential, channel conflict into something positive, change negative habits, and live in the moment.

3. ***Rich Dad Poor Dad*, Robert T. Kiyosaki:** It's been nearly twenty-five years since Robert Kiyosaki's *Rich Dad Poor Dad* first made waves in the personal finance arena. It has since become the number one personal finance book of all time, translated into dozens of languages and sold around the world. *Rich Dad Poor Dad* is Robert's story of growing up with two dads, his real father and the father of his best friend, his rich dad, and the ways in which both men shaped his thoughts about money and investing. The book explodes the myth that you need to earn a high income to be rich and explains the difference between working for money and having your money work for you.

4. ***Think and Grow Rich*, Napoleon Hill:** America's most beloved motivational author devoted twenty-five years to finding out how the wealthy became that way. After interviewing over 500 of the most affluent men and women of his time, he uncovered the secret to great wealth based on the notion that if we can learn to think like the rich, we can start to behave like them. By understanding and applying the thirteen simple steps that constitute Hill's formula, you can achieve your goals, change your life and join the ranks of the rich and successful. A great book writ-

ten in the 1930s and more relevant today than ever I believe.

5. ***Why We Sleep*, Matthew Walker:** Sleep is one of the most important aspects of our life, health and longevity and yet it is increasingly neglected in twenty-first-century society, with devastating consequences. Every major disease in the developed world—Alzheimer's, cancer, obesity, diabetes—has very strong causal links to deficient sleep. In this book, the first of its kind written by a scientific expert, Professor Matthew Walker explores twenty years of cutting-edge research to solve the mystery of why sleep matters. Looking at creatures from across the animal kingdom as well as major human studies, *Why We Sleep* delves into everything from what really happens during REM sleep to how caffeine and alcohol affect sleep and why our sleep patterns change across a lifetime, transforming our appreciation of the extraordinary phenomenon that safeguards our existence.

6. ***First Break All the Rules*, Marcus Buckingham:** The greatest managers in the world seem to have little in common. They differ in sex, age and race. They employ vastly different styles and focus on different goals. Yet despite their differences, great managers share one common trait: they do not hesitate to break virtually every rule held sacred by conventional wisdom. They do not believe that, with enough train-

ing, a person can achieve anything he sets his mind to. They do not try to help people overcome their weaknesses. They consistently disregard the golden rule. And, yes, they even play favourites. This amazing book explains why. This is one of my most referenced books to help people understand why they might not be happy at work and how to effectively help manage others.

7. ***How To Win Friends and Influence People*, Dale Carnegie:** Millions of people around the world have improved their lives based on the teachings of Dale Carnegie. This book offers practical advice and techniques, in his exuberant and conversational style, for how to get out of a mental rut and make life more rewarding. Reading this and applying learnings will turn your relationships around and improve your interactions with everyone in your life.

8. ***The 7 Habits of Highly Effective People*, Stephen Covey:** One of the habits, "start with the end in mind", is one of my most used phrases with my coaching clients. The author presents a holistic, integrated, principle-centred approach for solving personal and professional problems. With penetrating insights and pointed anecdotes, Covey reveals a step-by-step pathway for living with fairness, integrity, honesty and human dignity—principles that give us the security to adapt to change, and the wisdom and power to take

advantage of the opportunities that change creates. Fundamentals are the key to success. Stephen Covey is the master of them.

9. ***The Icarus Deception: How High Will You Fly?*, Seth Godin:** Readers are challenged to find the courage to treat their work as a form of art. Everyone knows that Icarus' father made him wings and told him not to fly too close to the sun; he ignored the warning and plunged to his doom. The lesson: play it safe and listen to the experts. It was the perfect propaganda for the industrial economy. What boss wouldn't want employees to believe that obedience and conformity are the keys to success? But we tend to forget that Icarus was also warned not to fly too low, because seawater would ruin the lift in his wings. Flying too low is even more dangerous than flying too high, because it feels deceptively safe.

    I had the privilege of attending the book launch as Seth brought the topic to life. Since before I can remember Seth has always inspired me since reading *The Purple Cow*—it was one of the inspirations for having the Blue Bean character made to bring the Student Beans brand to life when we launched back in 2005.

10. ***Atomic Habits*, James Clear:** Transform your life with tiny changes in behaviour, starting now. People think that when you want to change your life, you need to

think big. But world-renowned habits expert James Clear has discovered another way. He knows that real change comes from the compound effect of hundreds of small decisions: doing two push-ups a day, waking up five minutes early, or holding a single short phone call. He calls them atomic habits.

Leadership Programmes and Resources

Meltam: Meltam and now Masa make up a two-year leadership training course for years eleven and twelve which provides the opportunity to get equipped with all the skills needed to become a leader. Noam Masorti has been running this programme for over twenty years, creating young, capable, inspiring leaders for generations in our community. I did this programme when I was seventeen and it provided an incredible opportunity to learn foundational leadership skills, working in a team, leading by example and taking responsibility for others.

Young Enterprise (www.young-enterprise.org.uk/): Young Enterprise has over sixty years' experience creating and delivering opportunities for young people to apply their learning to real world contexts in the areas of enterprise, employability and financial education. It's the programme I did at school laying the foundations for Pion now the parent company of Student Beans which employs over 250 people.

AIESEC (https://aiesec.org/): As mentioned through various stories, AIESEC is a global platform for young people to develop their leadership potential through practical experiences of many kinds, including internships, volunteering opportunities, and more. From leading a team to my international experiences in the Philippines and Colombia it was just the most incredible life-changing experience. Founded in 1948, AIESEC is a non-governmental and not-for-profit organisation entirely run by youth for youth.

Charity: In the safety demonstration on an aeroplane they tell you to put your mask on first and then, if you can, help others around you. When you have your own bases covered there is nothing more rewarding than contributing to and helping others. I've mentioned the charities that have invested in me and that I give back in various ways including AIESEC, Meltam, and The King's Trust. I host the North London Cardiomyopathy UK support group helping bring together others in a similar position to me. Even if I am not feeling well, when I shift focus to helping others instead of focusing on my own troubles, my problems feel like they melt away. I helped a friend raise money for Cancer Research and nothing gave me more satisfaction than standing shaking my collection tin while asking for donations, smiling and complementing people as they walked past.

Back in 2010 I was at a Jewish Care fundraising event. There was a silent auction and you could write a bid on a piece of paper for the opportunity to have a business mentor—there were various entrepreneurs in the room offering their mentoring as part of the offer. A gentleman called Ian Simons stood up to introduce the concept of mentoring before the other mentors introduced themselves. Ian has a lifetime of experience coaching and mentoring CEOs, so I thought who better to mentor than someone whose profession it is. I bid and fortunately won and so started a relationship with Ian. I am so grateful for his time and support over the years. Whilst he's now retired we still catch up every so often. He's a true inspiration as he continues to live his life more fully than anyone I know from playing the piano to learning French literature, having an appreciation for the arts and music, always reading something new, and challenging me to be better. Thank you, Ian, for the help and support you've given me over the years.

What causes are close to your heart that you might be able to help raise some money for or give your time to?

Founders Pledge (https://www.founderspledge.com/): A London-based charitable initiative, where entrepreneurs commit to donate a portion of their personal proceeds to charity when they sell their business. Inspired by effective altruism, the mission of Founders Pledge is to "empower entrepreneurs to do immense good". I was inspired to make a pledge after hearing a number of entrepreneurs in my network be involved. David Goldberg the Co-Founder & CEO and alongside the team is passionate and driven helping people have the biggest impact with their charitable giving. As part of this community they regularly host events and trips to help bring this community together as well as deepening their impact. If you are a founder happy to share more about this, feel free to reach out or if you know any founders who you think might be interested feel free to share this with them.

The Yes Group (https://yesgroup.org/): Whilst I was a student at the University of Birmingham I was invited along to attend the local Yes Group community providing me the opportunity to network with like-minded people and be exposed to inspiring speakers.

Toastmasters (https://toastmasters.org/): To be able to speak confidently and publicly with others or on a stage is such a gift and there's no other organisation I've come across that trains and delivers this skill in such a practical way. With different chapters around the world, you can visit one local to you (and if there isn't one local perhaps you can look to set one up!). I attended a handful of events as a visitor, each time welcomed to a safe environment where you can learn and practise the art of public speaking and storytelling. You can sign up for different courses to perfect your speaking.

The Diageo High Performance Coaching Course: Experiencing the training directly from Diageo whilst I was in my final year of university gave me a real appreciation for coaching and the impact it can have on individuals and organisations.

The Naked Leader (https://www.nakedleader.com/): Through reading *The Naked Leader*, attending a number of events hosted by David Taylor and having the privilege to call him a mentor and friend over the years, he manages to cut through the buzzwords and helped me focus on showing up and bringing ideas into reality.

The Supper Club: (www.helmclub.co) Now known as Helm, The Supper Club was founded by Duncan Cheatle back in 2003 as a members club with a focus to help people connect over dinner to share experience and practical advice to help each other achieve their goals. Much has changed since the early days, but the principles and ethos remain. Duncan hosted a dinner for potential new members and whilst at the time we hadn't hit the one-million-pound-turnover threshold they opened the doors to a select few members—ones to watch. This presented an amazing opportunity as it meant that I was being surround by those in business who were that much further ahead than me. Despite being less experienced, whilst I was able to learn I was also able to contribute sharing new approaches we were taking and new technologies we were using that established businesses at the time weren't aware of being exposed to. Duncan has been a huge support for me and many people in the industry over the years including being one of the co-founders of Startup Britain. He also nominated me as a "changemaker" and a Startup Loan ambassador, another network that was invaluable as I grew my network and the business.

ICE (www.theice.network): Around five years into Student Beans I was introduced to Alex Hoye, an investor and entrepreneur, founder of Faction Skis as well as a co-founder of ICE. I was trying to set up a meeting with him—instead of meeting he said, "Why don't you join ICE's next ski trip?" ICE is a community like no other, more like a family. Made up of founders, investors and those committed to making the startup ecosystem thrive. Over the years I attended multiple ski trips, a summer trip to Croatia, Christmas parties and gatherings on roof tops. I remember one conversation with Alex when the business was only around fifteen people and we were growing and he said, "The people who got you here aren't necessarily the same people that are going to drive the next phase of the business, and that's OK." It was reassuring to hear and couldn't have been more true. Ultimately you need different people at different stages. If you're an entrepreneur in tech I'd highly recommend finding communities like this near you and if there isn't one, create one.

The Marketing Academy (https://themarketingacademy.org/uk/): A scholarship for those in marketing and entrepreneurs in the UK, USA and Australia. Through a combination of training, development, mentoring and coaching this immersive programme takes rocks and turns them into diamonds. As part of the programme all participants also experience The Living Leader programme, (https://www.thelivingleader.com/). I was fortunate enough to be trained by the founder, Penny Ferguson, who challenged and inspired us, breaking us down to build us back up. A special mention and credit also goes to Sherilyn Shackell the founder of The Marketing Academy who has worked tirelessly for the marketing community.

WaveLength (https://www.wavelengthleadership.com/): Founded by Adrian Simpson and Liam Black I participated in this programme on the back of finishing my scholarship with The Marketing Academy. Another fantastic opportunity where, as an entrepreneur, I got to mix with those in the corporate world, social housing initiatives, charities and other entrepreneurial best in class organisations. There were three residentials, amazing networking opportunities, learning, sharing and exposure to practical concepts that we were able to take back to The Beans Group to implement. Highlights included going to work at Pret a Manger for the day and going behind the scenes at Apple to understand how they deliver world-class products.

The DO Lectures (https://thedolectures.com/): Founders Clare and David Hieatt sparked the idea for the DO Lectures. The idea was a simple one: to gather together the world's DOers, disruptors and changemakers, have them share their hearts and stories, and encourage others to go and DO great things too. The event I attended was called DO Startup and all about getting people to start. It was an amazing three days in Wales, glamping, amazing food, singing around the fireplace and people. The thing about this event that makes it even more special is the speakers are attendees and very much positioned as equals participating alongside everyone else so we really got a chance to meet and know other attendees and speakers alike. I highly recommend attending in person if you get the chance. All of the talks are also shared freely online so have a look.

Landmark (https://www.landmarkworldwide.com/): Landmark is an internationally recognised personal and professional growth, training and development company with a community of more than 3.5 million graduates. I was introduced to the initial programme called The Landmark Forum by an old friend who recommended it. I attended an introductory meeting and thought, *What's the worst thing that can happen?* I attend for three days, spend some time reflecting on myself and have some time for myself. What I got was so much more. Focus and clarity on myself and why I do what I do and how to be more "me" and more fulfilled. I continued for fifteen months to do the advanced course and the Self Expression and Leadership programme as part of what they called the "curriculum for living". As you're reading this, if there's one course you want to explore that might help, I'd say this could be it. I did it in person, but it is also offered online.

Lifebook: During the summer of 2020 I discovered a programme created by Jon and Missy Butcher which was one of the programmes on MindValley (https://www.mindvalley.com/). Incidentally the founder Vishen Lakhiani was also an AIESECer. The programme has an amazing way of getting you to think differently and holistically around all the different areas of your life. Instead of simply asking what your vision is and what you are going to do about it (for example, be healthier means you will do more exercise), it adds another two layers to this. Firstly, what your premise and beliefs are around this area, then what your vision is, *then* why it is important, and finally the strategy you are going to employ to get there. From everything I have done it's the best combination of being clear around your beliefs (which indeed may be limiting you) as well as why it is important that keeps you focused and moving forward.

A tangible example for me was when my doctors said there is nothing day to day I can do that will help the situation with my heart. When I heard this I became quite disengaged, perhaps not surprisingly. When I did Lifebook and the beliefs around my health were questioned, it made me think about things that I am in control of, aka "the sphere of influence": what is within our control and what isn't. For me, I thought if I am going to need a heart transplant at some stage surely I should be as fit and healthy as possible going into that process which will help my recovery time. Similarly if I don't need the heart transplant within the timeframe they are suggesting, surely I want to be as fit and healthy as possible either way. From one day to the next,

I began my proactive focus on my health and fitness, doing yoga and walking or swimming where possible. If my beliefs are that I am a "healthy person" then this extends throughout my life and so, when shopping, I don't buy ice cream, for example (or at least less often!).

Meditation: Over the years I've always found the practice of meditation interesting. Whilst I ebb and flow with my consistency with it, I use a combination of methods today. For ease I often default to using www.calm.com which has a ten-minute daily meditation called the Daily Calm that I find a great structure to work with.

In August 2017 I did a transcendental meditation course for three days and was given my own mantra. I asked Naomi, who was delivering the course, the difference between guided and self-guided meditation and thought the answer was really interesting. Guided meditation can be easier; you listen to a voice which literally guides you through a meditation. If you are doing it alone it is up to you and your breath along with your awareness that takes you on the meditative journey. She said if you are always relying on an external stimulus you'll never be able to go as deep as if you are guiding yourself. However, guiding yourself is likely to take more practice and discipline. I can see the merits of both.

On another course a few years ago, the teacher shared a question they often get asked: "What is the best type of meditation?" The answer: "Any meditation that you do."

Another example of doing something is better than trying to wait for or find the "right" meditation.

Breathwork: Closely related to meditation, breathing, of course, is something we do all day every day. Often we get so caught up in the stresses of day-to-day life just taking a few minutes out to breathe and re-group can really make a difference. I'm not going to go into the science behind it (you can find out more I am sure) but all I know is it's good for you and often find it's one of those simple things. If you said you don't have time to do it, I would say you don't have time *not* to do it as by giving yourself a couple of minutes to focus on your breathing can help you focus and be much more productive. Here are a couple of exercises I wanted to share with you:

- Breathing the Box: Breathe in for four breaths, hold it for the count of four, breathe out for the count of four and hold your breath again for the count of you. Repeat this even just for a couple of minutes and you'll have more clarity and focus.

- Breathing Yourself To Sleep: In the past I would often struggle getting to sleep and one of the "tricks" I was taught on a course by Patrick McKeown (https://oxygenadvantage.com/) To fall asleep, it is about softening the breath – with a slow and gentle inhalation and a relaxed and slow gentle exhalation. It is about softening the breath to allow carbon dioxide to accumulate a little in the lungs and blood – to activate the rest and relax response. So simply, if you breathe in for three breaths and out for four breaths, you go to sleep. Try it and let me know how you get on! It's really so simple and transformed the way I get to sleep.

Journalling: There are various different approaches to journalling i.e. getting everything out of your head and writing. Not writing for the sake of writing a book or an article, but simply putting pen to paper or your fingers to a keyboard. There's something to be said for the transference of energy if you physically write something down. Whether it's in the morning first thing just to get everything out of your head so you are clear for the day, or at the end of the day, putting everything down that happened so you can head to sleep with a clean slate, there's value in both. One exercise is just to write until there is nothing else to write so you get the persistent thoughts and consciousness out on paper.

I wrote every day for six years when I started Student Beans. I look forward to sharing more of that one day in another book but that's for a different time.

Gratitude: You can't be sad and depressed whilst being happy and having gratitude. Often just stopping to reflect on what you are grateful for can make you feel happier. When I host various meet-ups I often finish with everyone attending, going around the circle and sharing what they got from the session and sharing what they are most grateful for. This could also be combined with journalling each day what you are grateful for.

Do You 10Q (https://www.doyou10q.com/): 10Q was inspired by the traditional ten days of reflection that occur between the Jewish holidays of Rosh Hashanah and Yom Kippur. This is a period of time that's long been considered an opportunity to look at where you're at, where you've come from, and where you're heading. Whether you're Jewish or not though, 10Q is a great free tool for anyone to look back at the year that's past, look ahead at the year to come, and take stock. That's a beautiful thing in any language. I do this myself and share it with my clients as the date sits at the end of September/October time each year so it's a good reference point with another three months or so before the end of the year, still providing time to take action or do things perhaps that you wanted to do, but for every reason life has got in the way. You can register your interest to get alerts when the vault is open again. Year after year it's inspiring to see the reflections and themes that come up, what's been achieved and what still needs to be done, what was important and what's important now.

Year Compass (https://yearcompass.com/): Year Compass is a free booklet that helps you reflect on the year and plan the next one. With a set of carefully selected questions and exercises, Year Compass helps you uncover your own patterns and design the ideal year for yourself. Learn from your mistakes, celebrate your victories and set out a path you want to walk on. All you need is a quiet few hours and the booklet. New year's resolutions don't work. Year Compass does—for more than a million people around the world since 2012. I've been using this myself and sharing it with my clients every year for the last few years. There are some elements and similarities for this and Lifebook—a great opportunity to reflect on the year gone and look forward to the year ahead. This can form a great blueprint for your future.

Therapy: Over the years I've had various forms of therapy, in person and online. I know a number of people who have found www.betterhelp.com to be useful. Traditionally there is a weekly structure for fifty minutes to an hour that gives you the opportunity to explore the past that might be causing you upset, or limiting your happiness, or what might be possible right now as well as exploring behaviours and patterns you might want to change. At the same time it could be for exploring grief or change in circumstances that are difficult to deal with alone or you don't feel comfortable sharing with friends or family. It can be a great safe space to discover more about yourself.

For me, chemistry is important as well as feeling like you can open up, be truthful and fully vulnerable with your therapist to get the most from the experience. The therapists I've found have always come through a recommendation, but there are lots of directories out there. Most (if not all) will offer an initial free call to understand what you are looking for, or an assessment session paid for without further commitment. Whilst it is an investment the importance of it can't be underestimated as well as the positive impact it can have.

Rapid Transformational Therapy: RTT was created by Marisa Peer. I had the pleasure of working with Manuel from https://www.heymanuel.com/ who trained with Marisa on RTT. Whilst there is, and can be, value in longer-term/structured therapy this was organised over three sessions, included a set-up and coaching call, hypnotherapy session and personalised recording and follow-up session. Extremely powerful, Marisa offers training now as well for Rapid Transformational Coaching and I had the pleasure of working with her team to provide feedback on the initial course design. Marisa still offers retreats and other opportunities to work directly with her and there are more and more people being trained with her work.

Coaching: As a coach myself, I value having my own coach. During my discovery calls as a coach I ask potential clients what the difference between coaching and therapy is, asking them to define what they understand each to be. As I see it there is a spectrum of support. Therapy looks back at the past and understands how experiences might have impacted you, and where it might be limiting you today and in the future. Coaching, however, is about looking to the future, setting goals, exploring what's possible and how you can be the best version of yourself. Both coaching and therapy have their place and are very powerful in their own right. At different times you may feel you need neither, either or both.

In *The Prosperous Coach* written by Rich Livitin, it says even if someone were to speak to a lamppost for an hour a week they would get value. Taking time and investing in yourself and your future can't be underestimated. With mental health being discussed more and more, having someone else to confide in and support you can be no bad thing. I've shared on LinkedIn and spoken out in the past that I think everyone should have a coach not just the CEOs or leaders in an organisation.

As with finding the right therapist, it is also important to have the right chemistry when finding and working with a coach. There are different types of coaches with different focuses and specialist fields, from life coaching to business coaching and everything in between. I position myself as a qualified work/life coach and business mentor, leading primarily with coaching so I am not a specialist.

Take your time, but don't worry about perfection if you don't find someone who resonates with you. Try them and if you like it and you feel you're getting value, carry on. If not, stop and try something else. The worst thing in my opinion you can do is identify you want some support but then don't decide to do anything about it as you can't find the "right" person. Sometimes a "breakthrough" happens when you just book something in and commit to something. That might be the thing that's holding you back! One thing to be aware of is coaching is not a regulated industry, so technically anyone can just say they are a coach. Of course, they might be great and have some great experience, but they might not have the necessary skills. A number of times the concept of coaching comes up and people call themselves a coach but they are actually a mentor. I will talk more about mentoring below. To finish here, just make sure you are clear with your aims and objectives of what you are looking for from a coach.

Optimus Coach Academy (https://www.optimuscoachacademy.com/): Optimus Coach Academy was founded by Ruth Kudzi, an amazing educational teacher championing coaching and the industry. If you like the idea of coaching and becoming a coach then this might be a great option for you. This could be a tool to complement what you currently do or indeed turn this into a full-time profession. Coaching is flagged as one of the fastest growing communities and demand is growing year on year as people and organisations continue to see the benefits.

Optimus Coach Academy is one of the world's leading coach training providers offering ICF accredited coach training that specialises in psychology- and scientific-based coaching approaches. I trained with them in 2021 becoming ACC ICF accredited. If you're interested in becoming a coach, feel free to contact me for an introduction to Ruth and as a bonus by signing up through me I can offer you a number of complementary coaching sessions and access to my ultimate coaching resource guide worth up to £1,000.

Mentoring: The idea of mentoring comes up time and time again. From a young age at school I was paired with someone older than me to help me navigate the transition to senior school. When I did Young Enterprise our team was given two mentors in business both of whom I'm still in touch with. The idea is getting insight from someone who has been there and done what you are trying to do or something similar, giving opportunities to seek advice and guidance. Over the years I've met thousands of people from all different walks of life. If you are looking for a mentor, my suggestion is simply to think about what it is you want to do and find others who have done it before. Attend events they might be attending or speaking at as often meeting in person can help get through the noise of simply connecting online. Failing that, reach out with a simple note applying the principles of the book; context is key as to why they might want to meet you. I've found often that when your interest is genuine and people are successful at the right time, they are keen to give back and help the next generation.

Health: Whilst I've touched upon all the things so far that are in line with supporting your personal and professional development, it's important to make sure you're supporting your body as well. Over the years, not simply because of my heart condition, I've been aware of the importance of looking after myself. Some of the treatments I've had include the Alexander technique, homeopathy, reflexology, acupuncture, reiki, osteopathy, massage and yoga. Of course, not all of these things at the same time but I list these things to shine a light on what support is out there. Pick and choose and explore what resonates with you. We often take our health for granted, I know I did. Ultimately if you don't have your health, what do you have?

Summary

This is the first time I've fully written and collated my personal development and leadership journey. On reflection, there's *a lot* there. With each programme came an increased depth of learning, building on some similar themes I'd come across and, of course, reminders of what I already knew. Some of it is common sense, but then as is often said, common sense isn't very common. The way I look at it is to ask myself each year what I am doing to invest in myself, and my personal development and growth. Alongside reading books and listening on Audible, how am I growing and challenging myself? What do you think would happen for you if you invested in yourself each year in this way?

When I was a coach on the Self Expression and Leadership programme with Landmark, we were running the final session with each of the attendees we were coaching. We were told to ask if the attendee had the support they needed to achieve whatever they were doing. That could be another course, a coach, trainer or teacher. For example, if they were looking to play the piano, did they have a piano tutor? Ever since, this has always stuck with me and whenever I've been in need, including writing this book, I've searched for the support I need to succeed. Do you have the support you need? If not, who can you ask and what could you put in place?

I've mentioned this in the context of finding a therapist or coach, but the same applies here. I'm surrounded by too many people who are struggling or stuck. They know they want things to change, they want a better life, they want a different job, to be living somewhere else, be healthier, be in a new or better relationship with others and/or themselves and yet they don't take action and they are waiting for the perfect course, perfect coach, perfect therapist, perfect solution to help them along the way. Waiting for the silver bullet, the one thing that's going to make everything better. Doing something is better than nothing, and ultimately it is the journey we are on, the experiences that we have, that is where living takes place.

Whilst these are various examples of things that you could or should do to help support your personal growth and development (and there are a multitude of stories and ideas), it is not simply about following what I have done. The aim is to help you see there is not simply one path, but to be inspired by these examples of how you can grow and collide more. We're all individuals with our own experiences and perspectives, but whoever you are, I want you to embrace the thinking in this book to not simply survive but thrive and succeed—whatever success means to you.

Life is what happens to you while you're busy making plans.
John Lennon

Part IV

Resources

Guides

Throughout the book I've shared stories of community initiatives and my general approach to networking. The guides that follow should help get you started creating collisions in the same way:

- How to network and make the most of attending events.
- How to help and make it easy for others to connect with you.
- A Facebook community group: the basis for Morzine Solos & Friends.
- A WhatsApp group: the basis for the community in my residential building.
- James' Introductory Declutter, Clear Out Guide.
- A monthly meet-up with sponsorship: the basis for Kentish/Camden Cluster.
- Icebreakers and engaging conversation starters.
- Connecting with people on LinkedIn.

- Writing directly to people.
- What you can send people to stand out.

How To Network at Events

1. Get there early. Be the first delegate to arrive; you can meet people as they come in. Clearly you can't all be the first but it is these moments at the beginning of the sessions that you have time and space to the connections that are otherwise missed.

2. Split up from your company. You can catch up with them when you are back home! By staying with your group you also sometimes make it harder for other people to connect with you so spread your wings!

3. Sit in a different place or on a different table every time, turning every session into another opportunity.

4. Don't be afraid to just #sayhello to everyone. Those amazing connections can come from where you least expect it—not just those on the stage.

5. Ask open questions e.g. What brings you here? What did you think of the last session? **Be the first to ask questions in the sessions** and have questions ready. What could you ask that can include information about your company or what you do? E.g. the head of marketing at Domino's—In your talk you said promotions were important. At Student Beans we know that student discounts are key, so how do you keep your offers fresh and engaging?

6. Netgiving. Instead of thinking about networking and what you can get, think about what you can give. Where can you add value? How can you help people? Think about the other person. What can you do to help them or connect them with someone else? Provide something. For example, a book reference, an article, a case study you can offer to send them which can be a great way of getting their email address (remember to follow up, e.g. would you like the slides to this presentation? If you give me your email address I can send them to you). Make sure you get their details, not just give them yours. It puts you in control.

Joining conversations when there is more than one person can sometimes be hard. Here are some tips to help you do just that:

7. Have a **look at the conversation** and ask the person who doesn't appear to be talking much if you can join the conversation. Simply asking, "Do you mind if I join you?" works well! (I know it sounds easy. It is. It just sometimes feels harder.)

8. Walk up to a group and **listen to the conversation** for a bit, and then make a contribution when it's appropriate.

9. Act like a host. If you see someone in the group without a drink, offer to get them one. It helps you to join the conversation when you get back.

The Collision Code

10. If you're in the group already, **make it easy for other people to join** and be aware of other people. Without realising it, people can exclude people very easily.

11. From an outside perspective, you may often think everyone already knows each other. It's only when you start speaking to people and ask if they know each other that you find out that **they only just met.**

There's only a limited time during the breaks and we've all been there. Sometimes we just get stuck with the same person and one or both of you might want to call it a day and speak to someone else but how do you get away? It happens to all of us. The next few tips are you help you move around more easily:

12. Fill your glass a quarter full so you can excuse yourself quickly and regularly to "get more drink" if need be! Only have a couple of things on your plate for the same reason.

13. In the conversation, just ask, "**Have you seen x person?** I've been looking for them." And excuse yourself to find them.

14. Honesty is also good so you can just say, "I'm sure you'll want to meet other people so I'll let you get on."

A final three more tips to keep you going…

15. If there's something useful during a conversation, **take a note on your phone** or write an action on his or her business card. This will help when you follow up afterwards. **Connect with people in real time too.** For example, cc them into an email with a relevant subject line and email yourself to make sure you follow up.

16. Use LinkedIn and/or post on x.com (formerly Twitter) to engage people and participate in the conversation using relevant #hashtags. Follow and connect with other people.

17. When all's said and done, **do follow up!** It's often that the opportunities are missed, not because you didn't meet but because the follow-up connection wasn't made.

* * *

How Can You Help and Make It Easy for Others To Connect with You?

Whilst I've shared a number of tips on how to network at events I thought it would be also useful to share some ideas as to how to make it easy or easier for others to connect with you whether that be at events or otherwise.

1. **Don't wear headphones in social settings.** It signals openness to conversation. By wearing headphones, it will dissuade people from speaking with you.
2. **Stand in open, welcoming postures.** Avoid crossing your arms or turning away.
3. **Put your phone away.** Look up; being present shows you're approachable.

4. **Wear something that sparks conversation.** A unique pin, hat, bright or interesting socks or shirt can be an easy icebreaker.
5. **Just say hello.** A simple greeting can open doors.
6. **Ask for help with something small.** People enjoy being helpful and it builds rapport.
7. **Compliment someone's specific choice.** Like their book, outfit or coffee order.
8. **Keep your facial expressions inviting.** Smile and avoid looking bored or distracted.
9. **Offer to share something.** A snack, a pen or a piece of advice.
10. **Show up early to events.** It's easier to start conversations before the crowd arrives.
11. **Ask "What's your story?" or a similar question.** It invites deeper sharing.
12. **Speak to the person who looks alone.** They might be hoping for someone to talk to.
13. **Leave space in group conversations.** Step back so others can join in.
14. **Be the first to introduce yourself.** Take the initiative in making contact.
15. **Remember small details and bring them up later.** It makes people feel valued.

16. **Sit in common areas.** Choose spots where interaction is natural.

17. **Offer a handshake or friendly wave.** Physical gestures help establish connection.

18. **Wear name tags at events when appropriate.** It breaks down barriers immediately.

Reflection Time: These are actionable and can be incorporated into everyday life. Which ones resonate most with you?

***

Creating a Facebook Community Group

If you Google "creating/running a Facebook community" you will be able to find lots of information, but I wanted to give you my version of a how-to. The key takeaway I want to leave with you is just *start*. Create one and you'll work it out. If it resonates and provides value, people will join. Try different things, see what works and what doesn't. The key is consistency in showing up (whether that be online or in person). Good luck and enjoy it.

1. **Search to see if anything currently exists** for what you are looking to create.

    a. If something exists, follow it, join it, show up if they have events in person and explore if it provides what you were looking to create.

b. If it doesn't exist, create a group. Make sure the title is easily searchable and obvious. There are group rules set as default that people need to agree to when joining. To make the group welcoming make sure you have a no soliciting/no selling policy. If people are found to be doing that, ask them to leave (or kick them out!).

2. **Invite a few people to join** who you know. If you don't know anyone, reach out to people on social media. When you meet people in person you can mention the group to them.

3. **Set up an auto welcome post** which tags everyone welcoming them to the group encouraging people to introduce themselves and share why they joined.

4. **Share events that are going on locally** you think people might be interested in.

5. If you are going to host events, **agree directly with individuals that you are going to meet up**, then you are definitely going to meet someone. If anyone else turns up then it's a bonus. Morzine Solos & Friends weekly drinks started like this. I hosted them weekly, and during the weeks I was busy I asked others to host who had shown up and valued the community— it's important to be able to trust others.

6. At events **having a host is key**. Wear something identifiable so people can easily find you. Choose a

bright colour and, if you want to, invest in a branded T-shirt/jumper.

7. **Don't worry about the design** to begin with, but as you grow you might want to invest some more time in it. Tools like Canva are great and simple to use (https://www.canva.com/) or you could always get someone on Fiverr (https://www.fiverr.com/) to do a logo, headers, etc. or better yet get someone in the community to contribute by doing some design work.

8. Often people say to me, "Why don't you organise a meet-up on this topic or theme?" As I don't want the community to be reliant on one person I push back and **suggest if they want to organise something it's up to them** to put it out and share.

9. Initially I let anyone post anything on groups, but as they grew they started to get more and more spam. If this happens **you can put post approval on and get people to answer questions** when they apply to be part of the group. There is some admin for this, but it's made a big difference. At the time of writing, Morzine Solos & Friends will hit almost 4,000 members so since there's value in joining, those barriers don't put the right people off.

* * *

Creating a WhatsApp Group for Your Community/Building

As mentioned in one of the stories, years before this was common practice, I created a WhatsApp group for everyone who lived in my building (twenty-five different flats). Again, there will be guides online covering what you need to do but this is my how-to:

1. **Create the group, add a picture of the building and short description.** Example: This group is for all residents, leaseholders, tenants who live in xxxxxxxx. It is a group chat to help each other with everything from sharing parking spaces to sharing leftover food ⌧ (and anything in between). Request: only replies relevant to everyone should be sent to all. Otherwise if people can help with specific requests, you can click on the person who sent the original message and reply privately.

2. **Knock on doors and introduce yourself**, sharing you've set up the group. You can also write a note to leave in their post box/pigeonhole/under the door. Example: My name is xxxx I've recently moved in/I've been living here for a while and a friend suggested/I read in this book that a WhatsApp group has made a real difference for the community they live in so I thought I'd set one up and get everyone involved. The aim of the group is simple: to share

information or help each other/ask for help informally and easily. To be part of the group simply drop me a message on WhatsApp xxxxxxxxxx and I'll add you in.

Often when I share the story and encourage people to set something like this up more often than not they say that a group would never work in their building as there are a couple of really annoying people who would always complain. Don't let that stop you. Don't overthink it. As before, my advice is just start, and if people do get troublesome you can always give them a warning that if they carry on they will be removed. From my experience the benefits far outweigh any negatives and really have made such a difference to the community I live in.

***

James' Introductory Declutter Clear out Guide:

Tips & What I should have done at the beginning of the clear out:

eBay: If you don't have one immediately create an ebay account. This means you are already to sell when it comes to it. It can be helpful to buy some things on ebay to start building up your feedback rating which will help when you start selling.

It seems to be common to choose a very random name for your profile - perhaps so you can't be identified could also be useful for example if you're selling random gifts that you don't want people to know you're selling them on!

I decided to put the starting price at a level that I'd be happy to accept if there was just one bid.

You can also do a search and filter the results to see the price your item previously sold for which gives a good indication of what you might get.

Be as clear as possible in your description where any scratches are, if there is no charger etc. It's amazing what sold, even old computers that didn't turn on I listed for parts only and sold for £80.

The clear out;

1. Work section by section starting furthest from the front door.
2. Take everything out of the cupboard / draw / shelf and only put back in what you want to keep.
3. Only put what you want to keep in that place otherwise put it in the keep box.
4. Have 3 boxes - definitely keep, definitely give and a maybe. If you are unsure about something, put it in the maybe pile / box.
5. Whilst you are going through the process the mess might get worse before it gets better. If boxes don't work, create zones in the biggest space you have available to you.
6. Once you've decided what you are going to keep every so often go back to the maybe area and repeat

the process. You could also give yourself a time limit for example if you haven't used it in 6 or 12 months then you will get rid of it.

7. I'd recommend going through everything first once and everything you want to get rid of it together. There are examples when I sold something and then I found the charger later in another cupboard which is why it's best to go over everything at once and organise everything you want to get rid of.

8. Once you have everything together it's now time to find out what you've got in your 'shop', what you want to sell and what you should give away or take to a charity shop.

9. It might be worth doing the search on eBay first even if you think it has no value.

10. Go through each item if you're happy to just give it away, group it together and either take it to a charity shop if you think there's a good chance they can sell it. Or start listing on OLIO or other Freecycle Apps / websites.

Getting Selling:

1. Some items it can be useful to share the original price for example there was a watch I had that was a bit scratched, usual wear and tear but in good condition, the battery wasn't working it originally cost

around £150 - I shared an image of the watch selling for new and I ended up selling it for £35. I got over £60 in total for 5 watches I thought there was nothing I could do with.

2. Take photos of everything with a neutral background - as many photos as possible that reflect the item in a good but honest light.

3. If you list everything on the same day then if you are allowing people to bid the listings will end at a similar time so you can pack up and post whatever has sold all at the same time.

4. Ending sales on a Sunday evening seems to be a good time when things sell.

5. ebay has a great re-listing function so if you haven't been lucky the first time round it will keep re-listing it to save you time and you can also agree for the price to be slightly lowered each time.

6. When you list an item make sure you charge correctly for the postage if you want to charge separately for it. You can put free P &P but of course you need to absorb the costs in the sale. The Royal Mail have put up their prices in January so to send a small parcel 2nd class signed for costs £4. Inpost comes in slightly cheaper at £3.63 but then you don't need to queue up. At the beginning if you are unsure go to the post

office with a packed up item asking if you send it in the UK with tracked delivery how much will it be?

7. Once you sell you can use the postage option to prepay or again if you are unsure on pricing to begin with, I just went to the post office and put it on the scale and asked the price and worked it out over the first few times.

8. If you know you're going to be doing a clear out start keeping padded envelopes and boxes along with any packaging so you are all ready to go once the sales start.

9. As soon as you've sold an item and you've been paid - get it securely packaged up. I'd wait until you get paid as a couple of times I wasn't paid and the buyer just went quiet so I had to re-list the item.

10. Out of all the platforms when you are selling I like eBay best due to the security it provides both the buyer and seller.

11. When I started selling on ebay with a new account there was a limit on selling a maximum of 10 items in a month. I contacted the support within a couple of minutes on the chat & explained I was doing a big clear out and it would be a big help if this limit was increased which they did immediately - so definitely worth asking.

Postage:

There are some great postage options that you can buy through eBay so you can print the labels and have a courier pick up your parcels instead of needing to go to the post office.

It's also sometimes cheaper to use InPost where you can drop off at a locker so you don't need to wait the whole day for a courier to pick up and you don't need to go inside or stand in any queues. They work with other couriers to do deliveries.

It's always good to get tracked deliveries so you know the items have arrived and they are insured. You can also use DPD.

I've still got some way to go. There are a number of places online that you can use and go to to support your clear out and minimalist lifestyle these include;

Vinted - Don't wear it? Sell it! Set your price and sell with 0% fees. Plug - Click on the link - download the app to start selling your clothes & accessories in this specialist online market place; https://www.vinted.co.uk/invite/blue2976 use my link.

Ziffit - Money for your Books, Games, DVDs & CDs - Perhaps not a lot but it all adds up pennies makes pounds as they say! It's a good way to get rid of them easily and https://

www.ziffit.com/en-gb/donate-my-stuff - just scan the barcode and off you sell.

Music Magpie - sell electronics, DVDs, Games, Lego books & more - similar to Ziffit but worth comparing the two as I found different prices on each of the platforms. https://www.musicmagpie.co.uk/ like Ziffit - just scan the barcode and off you sell.

Thrift Plus - Sell your branded clothing on here, make money & raise money for charity. You get a Thrift Bag and send off your clothes; they do the rest. If they can't sell something they donate it themselves. https://thrift.plus/

***

Creating a Way To Bring the Local Community Together

This was the process I went through to create the Kentish Cluster:

1. **Search to see if anything currently exists** for what you are looking to create.

    a. If something exists, follow it, join it, show up if they have events in person and explore if it provides what you were looking to set up.

    b. If it doesn't exist, create a group either on Facebook or Instagram. Make sure the title is easily searchable and obvious.

2. Before inviting people to the group, **define what it is**. What are its objectives?

3. **Invite people to the platform** you've chosen to host the community. A good idea which we did for Kentish Cluster was to have founding supporters in the form of established businesses, which meant between all our companies involved there were already over 200 or so employees.

4. **Have an event on a regular schedule**: once a month, or once a quarter

    a. Speak to venues, actually go in and ask to speak to a manager or owner and explain you are hosting something for the community and you'll promote them. No venue charged us despite having a usual booking fee.

    b. Ask them if they are able to provide the first drink for free. Bars can often get a brewery or drinks company to subsidise/provide something. Once we had a sponsor to cover drinks instead, I would ask the venue if, instead, they could give us a special price on a few drinks to keep people around longer—more often than not they did.

5. For the event:

    a. Choose a platform like Eventbrite (https://www.eventbrite.com/) where people can register for a ticket. There are different formats, from completely free (you might get more registrations and more people might not turn up) to paid. Fifty percent is a reasonable show rate for free events. You could also charge something which could include a first drink. Or just charge something to make money or have a charity partner or a combination of the above. There is no right or wrong way but depending on the audience they will respond differently.

b. Be early!

c. Have a banner and/or wear something that's easily identifiable so people can find you.

d. Have name badges. It helps people know who is at the event and meet each other more easily.

e. If you are giving a free drink, **you'll need some form of token for people to exchange at the bar.** Raffle tickets are a simple solution, or print something small like the name of the community or the logo if you have one, and laminate them so they can be reused. Give these to people as they arrive.

6. **Sponsorship:** Think about who might like to get in front of the community you are bringing together. As we were focused on businesses and people who live and work in the area, our business landlords agreed to put in some money. Think about what's in it for

them and what you want from them. It might just be sponsorship in kind i.e. a venue space and drinks, rather than money too.

7. **Charity:** Consider having a charity partner. This is a great way to engage with the community and give back. The charity might also have a venue you can use and other ways you might be able to partner together.

8. **PR:** Partner with a local PR company and/or publication. This might be online or, if there's one in print, the local newspaper. It's a great opportunity for them to raise their awareness with the community and connect with people and businesses. They'll also be able to invite their advertisers and clients to events. You can also use some of the sponsorship money to print adverts or include flyers with the distribution.

Here are the example documents used from Kentish/Camden Cluster:

Kentish Cluster

Camden Cluster

Sponsorship Proposal December 2015

History

The Beans Group moved to Kentish Town in November (2013) and have since discovered a number of great businesses in the area and thought it was about time that we said hi and got together. A few of us then started talking and thought there'd be an opportunity to formalise the cluster of businesses in the area and so the idea of Kentish Cluster was born. We successfully grew and subsequently established Camden Cluster to develop our presence further afield.

A quarterly event is hosted in Kentish Town and in the months in between in Camden Town.

What Is Kentish Cluster/Camden Cluster?

The group/cluster of organisations and people who work in Kentish Town/Camden Town area. Whilst there's a focus on tech companies, with digital playing such a big part in many businesses today, everyone is welcome.

Objectives of Kentish Cluster/Camden Cluster:

- to put Kentish Town on the map as a hub and destination
- to provide a hub and support for organisations and people working in Kentish Town/Camden Town

- to help people who live in the area find jobs reducing their commute and increasing the community feel for the area.

What's the Point?

We're all working hard and bring a lot to the area. We thought it would be a good idea to get together and meet everyone and have a drink, say hi and take it from there. We think there's maybe more we can do and help each other with but we thought let's start with monthly drinks.

Who's Involved?

We've got a few locals involved who have been here a little and some a lot longer than us, who can help spread the word and we can make this all happen together.

Founding Supporters of Kentish Cluster Include:

James Eder - www.wearepion.com

Xxxxx

Charity partner for both Kentish and Camden Cluster: The Roundhouse (roundhouse.org.uk)

The Plan

Over the next twelve months the aim is to:

1. have reached out and connected with all of the local businesses and engaged with them on social media

and built a comprehensive email list.
   - currently xxxxx people
   - companies currently include: xxxxxxx
2. have grown and held a monthly drinks each month. Room for a bigger event at Christmas and summer.
3. have a consistent PR campaign amplifying all the Kentish Cluster and Camden messages and great work we're all doing.

Sponsorship Opportunity

To help the ecosystem we are looking for a limited number of organisations to help support and grow the Camden and Kentish Cluster community.

For a monthly fee of £500 over the next twelve months a headline sponsor will receive the following:

- subsidising the first couple of drinks at the monthly drinks
- inclusion in the three monthly emails:
  - the thank you message for attending
  - the mid-month reminder
  - last reminder a couple of days before
- weekly social media inclusions and mentions on Twitter and re-tweets
- flyers put out at the event and a print of 20,000 flyers

to be distributed to local businesses and homes

- local press monthly feature profiling the sponsor in a favourable light. TBC story, angle, etc.
- PR—maximising the opportunity we will collaborate with a local firm to deliver a PR campaign working closely with a local publication
- feature on our website
- feature on our popup banner that will be displayed at all events
- Monthly PPC Facebook/Instagram ads.

The money raised will be spent directly on the above activities.

The headline sponsor will receive first refusal on any additional sponsorship opportunities.

For any questions please feel free to speak to James on xxxxxxxx.

James Eder
Founding Supporter
Kentish Cluster/Camden Cluster

The Collision Code

Proposal agreement example that can be adjusted and personalised:

Kentish Cluster

Date

For a monthly fee of £500 plus VAT per month over the next twelve months a sponsor will receive the following:

- subsidising the one or two drinks at the monthly drinks (subject to attendance and capacity)
- inclusion in the three monthly emails:
    o the thank you message for attending
    o the mid-month reminder
    o last reminder a couple of days before.
- monthly social media inclusions and mentions on FB and Twitter
- supporting the founders/MD quarterly meet-up subsidising a meal/drinks
- coverage in local media TBC how that would look on- and offline
- PR—maximising the opportunity we will deliver a PR campaign working closely with local media

- small logo inclusion on the flyers put out at the event and a print of 5,000 flyers to be distributed to local businesses
- small logo inclusion on the popup banners to be used at events.

The Sponsor understands that:

- all of the sponsorship money contributed will be spent on initiative benefiting Kentish Cluster, the people and organisations in the area
- the contribution of £500 plus VAT per month is for an agreed minimum of twelve months. This is with a view to growing and supporting the Kentish Cluster ecosystem.
- Kentish Cluster will be open to working with **the sponsor** to maximise the partnership and open to suggestions as it grows but will ultimately decide the best place to allocate the sponsorship based on the outline above.

Signature:	Signature:
_____	_____
Kentish Cluster	**(The Sponsor)**
Print Name:	Print Name:
Date:	Date:

***

Icebreakers

When hosting a dinner, a great game and way to get to know each other instead of just asking for introductions is "two truths and one lie". Each person goes in turn making a statement of two things that are true and one thing that is a lie. The others need to discuss and decide who thinks which statements are truthful and which is the lie. For example:

1. I met Princess Diana when I was five years old and gave her some flowers.
2. I am one of four children.
3. I spend up to six months a year living in France.

If you, as the host, go first it gives people the opportunity to think of something. Whenever I have done this at the beginning it can be a bit slow to take off but when people have thought about what they want to share people can't wait for their turn and want to go next. It provides stimulation for further conversations and brings up discussions that a simple introduction wouldn't necessarily invoke.

***

Other questions you could ask for engaging conversation starters:

- If you could only live in one country for the rest of your life, where would you live?
- If you could only eat one type of food, what would it be?
- If you could travel anywhere in the world right now, where would you go and why?
- What are you reading right now? What's your favourite book?
- What's the most memorable meal you've ever had, and what made it so special?
- What book/movie/TV show had a significant impact on you and changed your perspective?
- If you could have dinner with any historical figure, who would it be?
- What's a skill or hobby you've always wanted to learn but haven't had the chance to yet?
- What was the best piece of advice you've ever received, and how did it influence your life?
- If you could live in any time period, past or future, which would you choose and why?
- If you could instantly master any talent or skill, what would it be and how would you use it?

- What cause or issue are you passionate about? How can we make a difference?

***

Short LinkedIn Request

The key here is to keep it short and to the point.

Dear xxxxx,

I recently read an article about the great work you've done. As I'm starting out my career I'm keen to follow in your footsteps and wondered if you could spare thirty minutes to share some of your advice. Happy to visit you at your offices or somewhere convenient. If it's easier we can do a virtual coffee on Zoom.

Many thanks,
James

Writing Directly to People: Request To Meet Someone in Person

Remember people are people just like you and me they have aspirations, dreams and desires. If you don't ask, you never know. Warm introductions are, of course, likely to get a better response rate.

This was the actual email I used to write to David Taylor (who wrote the foreword of this book) and his response to my email is below.

—Original Message—

From: James Eder
Sent: 26 August 2003 05:25
To: David Taylor
Subject: Thank you for writing!

Dear David,

I hope you are well. My name is James Eder. I am currently in the Philippines working for an organisation called AIESEC. Originally from London, I am entering my second year at the University of Birmingham.

One of my closest friends dropped me at the airport on 1 July. Leaving me standing outside the shop, she disappeared to go and buy me something. She returned with your book, saying it seemed very me.

Just over eight weeks later, after a very challenging time here, I started reading your book last week and finished it within days. I know I will have to read through it again and probably a few more times after that to get the most from your book.

I am a true believer in many of the things you said. Knowing where you want to go is something I truly value. An example I used while talking with a group of people—even if you have a map—if you don't know where to go, you are still lost.

AIESEC's core work is facilitating an exchange programme working in over eight-four countries and organising suitable work placements between two and eighteen months for recently graduated students.

One of the reasons I am writing to you apart from to thank you for your book is to ask if you would be interested in meeting and possibly working with AIESEC in the UK. We are based in twenty-three universities and throughout the year hold conferences and events where we are constantly in need of motivational speakers. The organisation is also "developing the future leaders of tomorrow". Through the organisation, students gain a practical working knowledge and understanding of working in a team: leadership, management and marketing skills.

For additional general information about the organisation you can look at www.aiesec.org.

I return to England, London on 2 September and would be very interested in meeting with you.

I hope that you might consider working with us or at least we are able to have an introductory meeting at your convenience.

I look forward to hearing from you soon.
Yours sincerely
James Eder

From: David Taylor
Sent: 27 August 2003 16:39
To: James Eder
Subject: RE: Thank you for writing!

Dear James

Thank you for writing to me, and also for your kind comments about the book, which are really appreciated.

The success of the book has changed my life completely, and I am now very busy touring the world as it is published, and filming a new TV series. However (and this is where you thought I was going to say no to working with AIESEC!) I would love to speak at one of your events. Indeed, I am very keen to look at ways of getting the message of being the very best that you already are to as wide a community as possible.

I will e-mail some possible dates when we can meet.

With very best wishes,

David
Imagine if you simply could not fail:
What would you do?
Where would you go?
Who would you be?
Be the very best that you already are
www.nakedleader.com

Writing Directly to People: Getting an Introduction Through a Referral

Whilst this may be harder when you are starting out, getting someone else to ask for you can get a better response. For example:

Dear xxxx,

I see you are connected with xxxxx. As I'm starting out my career or looking to understand more about the industry I was wondering if you could introduce me to them to set up a thirty-minute meeting or call to get some advice.

Many thanks,

James

Getting Someone's Attention Through the Post

Make sure you have the right address then:

- send a handwritten letter
- send something by FedEx
- send a personalised chocolate bar
- send a tea bag suggesting they have a cup of tea whilst they read your proposal/CV
- Send a WISPA chocolate bar and say, "I heard a 'wispa' you were recruiting." Or some other fun phrase, depending on what you are reaching out for.

- A lottery scratch card. We sent these one year with our January New Year's cards saying, "A little something, that could be a big something. Season's greetings, we hope you have a great year ahead."
- A book. Either one you've published or another that you thought they'd appreciate.

In this day and age, you can try using AI (e.g. ChatGPT) to get ideas. Don't simply copy and paste the responses but use them to help and guide you.

I asked if it could provide me with an email address for me and it replied with the following:

I can't provide personal contact details like email addresses, but I can suggest other ways to reach out to James Eder:

LinkedIn: *Connect or send a message through his LinkedIn profile. Many professionals are active on LinkedIn, and it's a good platform for networking.*

Company Website: *Visit the Student Beans website and use their contact form or general inquiries email. You can mention that your message is intended for James Eder.*

Social Media: *Look for his presence on platforms like Twitter or Instagram, where you might be able to send a direct message or engage with his content.*

Networking Events or Conferences: *If you're in the industry, attending events where he might be speaking could provide an opportunity to connect in person.*

These methods are respectful and effective ways to reach out to someone you're interested in connecting with.

Acknowledgements

Thank you to everyone who has been part of my journey and contributed—directly or indirectly—to this book, which has taken years to write. There's a saying: people come into your life for a reason, a season, or a lifetime. If we've crossed paths and I haven't mentioned you by name, please know that the omission is unintentional. I am grateful for you and the role you've played in my journey. With that, here goes.

Firstly, my family: Diana (Mum) for being the constant calm, the alternative view, the one who gives the perspective that no one else sees. I'm so grateful for your love and support.

Bernard (Dad) for always believing in me, giving me the support to forge my own path, fail and learn and pick me up when things don't work out. You have always given us children advice and at the same time supported us when we make different decisions but I know always you want us to be happy, and to let you know, I am. Claire, thank you for being there and supporting Dad and softening some of my adventurous stories and updates to make them easier for him to digest!

To my brothers and sister, their partners, and my nieces and nephews: Simon, Sharon, Anaya, Jonah, Livi, Michael, Steph, Toby, Mia, Hannah, Andy, Noah, Jesse River, Sage,

Ben, Anna and Dylan. What an amazing collection of people you all are. Each time I see you I am continually amazed with your energy and passions from sports to music and everything in between.

To my teachers, therapists and coaches who have worked, challenged and supported me over the years. From my school years: Miss Jaia, Hampstead Hill School, Andrea Taylor, Mary, Jean, Joan, Ida, University College School, Mrs Thomas, Miss Spencer, Mrs Beagle, Mr Hubbard, Mr Youlden, Mr Haggar, Mr Durham, Mr Chapman, Mr Bowes-Jones, Miss Dolata, Mr McAra, Mr Roberts, Mr Bateman, Mr Hawkins, Mr Smith and Mrs Beadle.

To those who had conversations with me about writing this book with each conversation a stepping stone to the next, Rachel Davies, John Monks, Cate Caruth, Matthew Stafford, Katie Lewis and Robbie Dale.

To those who are in the book David Taylor aka The Naked Leader, Dame Julia Cleverdon, Anthony Eskinazi, Musa Tariq, Neil Chauhan, Leanne Hoffman, Nicola Garcia, Brent, Danielle, Chloe, Jocelyn, Sandy, Zied, Tony Brown, Andrew Katz, Alex Singer, Lionel Simons, Derek and Maggie Small, Jaime Augusto Zobel de Ayala, Andrea Elliot, Suzanne Worthington, Juan Milford, Dan Tatnall-Murray, James Shaw, Dave Clearwater, Tom Hughes, Majken Rønne, Dr Samuel (Sammie) Mwaura, Damian Drabble, Emma Rees, Terry Murphy, Eugénie Harvey, Lord Bilimoria, Sahar Hashemi OBE, Gary Beckwith, Stephen Grabiner, Hum-

Acknowledgements

phrey Black, Dave Lewis, Emily Aviss, Mark Beardmore, Victoria Barclay, Paul Birch, Michael Acton Smith, Poonam Sakarsudha, Lord Young, James Cann, Bev James, Duncan Cheatle, Carrie Green, Jodie Cook, Richard Hurtley, Kate Robertson, David Jones, Sir Bob Geldoff, Sir Richard Branson, Professor Muhammad Yunus, Arianna Huffington, Paul Polman, Ella Robertson, Prof Rajiv Joshi, Daniel Priestley, Fraser Doherty, Jonathan Conway, Rob Allison, Amanda Harris, Luke Mitchell, Richard Jackson, Steven Bartlett, Sherry Coutu CBE, Reid Hoffman, Emmanuel Gavert, Gregor Lawson, Craig McCoy, James Hart, Zak Sos, Carolyn McCall, Jon Goldstone, Penny Ferguson, Sherilyn Shackell, Russ Lidstone, Lisa Faulkner, Ben Shepherd, Sarah Ellis, Laura Hagan, Adam Rostom, Tammy Potter, Simon Biltcliffe, Ita Murphy, Amanda Mackenzie OBE, Shaa Wasmund MBE, Oli Barrett, David Hieatt, David and Kathryn Allen, Edward Lamont, Nick Johnston, William Harris, Darren Ziff, Sam Conniff, Angus George, Olivia Newman, Simon Kay, Elliot Moss, Matt Kingdon, Nick Fine, Emilia Grala, Priscila Finkler Innocente, Hugo, Pag, Andrew Monchar, Guy and Gabi Soudry, Chris Wilson, Rory Sutherland, Titus Sharpe, Oleg Efrem, Eric Ries, Dennis Xenos, Matt Clifford, Michael Langley, Christine Lai, Andrew Webster, Edward Prendergast, Sharon Graham, Bernard Adams, Clémence Dumas, Lorraine Peters, Andrea Petherbridge, Pavlos Grivas, Thomas and Penny Power, Ryan Mathie, Simon Franks, Robin Alvarez, Brett Akker, Mike Butcher MBE, Julia Hobsbawm OBE, Derek Draper, John Davy, Marisa Peer, David Remmington, Grace Lynskey, Jim Lynskey, Emma Jones, Adrian Simpson, Liam Black, Clare and David Hieatt, Vishen Likhani, Jon and Missy Butcher, Patrick McKeown, Naomi Wright, Manuel Schlothauer, Ian Simons, Ruth Kudzi, Alex Hoye and David Goldberg. The Morzine Solos & Friends Community including Jenny, Liz, Nigel, Hannah, Gráinne, Ben, Rhiannon, Morag, Stephen, Kathy & Stephen, Jon and the Johns, Maria, Natan, Lorna, Tom, Tommy and many more who have joined and contributed to the community over the years.

To friends and extended family who have been part of the journey and really made a difference for me: Andrew and Rosina Eder, Shirley and Kenny Schreiber, Charlotte Eder, Vivien and Philip Eder, Charlotte Koelliker, Christina de Poitiers, Gemma Marks, Lucy Morgan, Georgie Maddock, Susie Lenton, Kate Barker, Sarah Lloyd Hughes, Daniel Ruby, Paul Thomas, Jon Shuster, Benjamin Black, Robin Abrams, Pippa Shenkin, Matt Kepple, Naomi Russel, Claire Starbuck, Caroline Brown, Helen Laidlaw, Becky Dean, Vanessa Towers, Marielle Fillit, Andrew Henry, Des Rowlinson, Sam Feller, Elliot Leslie, Joseph Lin, Andrew Carr and Dina Pinner.

Finally to the whole Cardiac Team at The Royal Free Hospital, St Bartholomew's Hospital and Royal Papworth Hospital who have looked after me over the years and continue to look after and support me—you are incredible people, thank you.

What people are saying about James Eder's *The Collision Code*

There are life-changing moments just waiting for you and they can be unlocked if you have the confidence to simply say "hello". In *The Collision Code* James shares not only inspiring examples from his life but also the frameworks and tips you can use to immediately have a go at connecting with people. Please do it—and keep doing it—you never know where that "hello" might lead.

Matthew Stafford, Co-Founder of 9others, Author of Find Your 9others, *Investor at stafford.vc*

The Collision Code reveals the transformative power of everyday interactions, showing how simple moments can lead to extraordinary opportunities. The themes and stories resonate especially due to the nature of our 9others dinners and events—where strangers become part of a community and collaborators.

Katie Lewis, Co-Founder of 9others, Author of Find Your 9others, *Co-Founder and COO of Aspire*

Where others see dead ends, James finds doorways. He has a gift for turning chance encounters and unexpected collisions into golden opportunities. James taught me that the most powerful connections are often the ones you stumble upon. This book is about how to master the accidental opportunity.

William Harris, Chief Revenue Officer at Pion!

James' story is a profound reminder of how precious life is and the urgency of truly living. The Collision Code is more than a book, it's a wake-up call. In our fast-paced digital world, where connection often feels more distant than ever, this book offers the inspiration and guidance we all need to feel more fulfilled, present, and alive. James challenges us to stop waiting for the 'right time' and start making meaningful collisions, embracing the moments, relationships, and opportunities that shape a life well-lived. A must-read for anyone who wants to live with more purpose, intention, and heart.

Carrie Green, Founder, Female Entrepreneur Association

The Collision Code offers powerful insights into building unexpected connections. It's an inspiring read to help you expand your network and uncover new opportunities in creative ways.

Simon Kay, Senior Account Director at Geiger

The Collision Code gets what I know to be true: random moments change everything. But James breaks spontaneity down into practical steps we can all use daily. He knows that train conversations can become clients and overheard words can spark business pivots. Read this book to tap into the secrets of serendipity and create your own luck.

Jodie Cook, Founder of Coachvox. Senior contributor at Forbes

The Collision Code is a deeply insightful reflection into how to make massively meaningful connections. A must-read for anyone looking to make impact.

Titus Sharpe, Founder of MVF

Meeting James through The Prince's Trust back in 2005, there was something unique about James' approach. *The Collision Code* demystifies how to connect with those around you giving you everything you need to succeed and build your network.

Dave Lewis, Former Prince's Trust Business Manager

The Collision Code offers practical insights to build meaningful connections and unlock opportunities for innovation and impact.

Prof Rajiv Joshi, Founder of Bridging Ventures

The way I met James, on a stage at an event, how he offered me a lift in his car and then how he was featured on a segment I did for Reuters TV is a real example of *The Collision Code* in action. This is a must-read helping you to unlock opportunities that surround us every day.

Zak Sos, Reporter at KTVU Fox 2 News

James from his school days was never driven by greed but by the desire to help others by showing how it can be done and to always look forward. *The Collision Code* shows other people a way and what's possible.

Andrew Haggar, Former Teacher and Young Enterprise Lead

The Collision Code is a compelling reminder that serendipity often plays a pivotal role in success. Being open to sudden opportunities, and having the confidence to seize them, can make all the difference. An insightful perspective on how the right mindset can transform unexpected moments into defining ones.

Ella Robertson McKay, Managing Director, One Young World, Author of "How To Make A Difference"

Throughout my career it is the connections I've made that make everything possible. The Collision Code makes meaningful interactions accessible to everyone.

Stephen Grabiner, Private Equity Investor, Former Media Executive

The Collision Code is a fascinating look at the power of serendipity and connection. Insightful and thought-provoking, it will change how you see chance encounters and hidden opportunities!

Rachel Davies, ACC, Leadership Coach

When I was asked to help develop The Collision Code, I jumped at the chance. At Today Do This, we help people turn intent into action in order to make a positive impact on the world, and few embody that philosophy better than James. I hope his story, and his particular way of looking at life, will inspire positive action for years to come.

Robbie Dale, Co-Founder at Today Do This

Behind every business is the coming together and connection of people that can really make or break it. *The Collision Code* shines a light on how to make connections where you'd least expect them and is a great read for any founder looking to build a network that drives success.

Tom Hughes, Founder of Milkround and Entrepreneur

The Collision Code helps readers unlock potential opportunities that surround us every day. A great read to help you think differently about connecting with people.

Majken Rønne, Head of E-Commerce at On AG

Reading *The Collision Code* made me reflect on my own journey. It reminded me that every connection, every experience, and every challenge holds meaning, even if it's not immediately clear. James' ability to find purpose in the past and weave it into the present is really inspiring. His insights highlight how relationships and experiences—past, present and even future— hold meaning and are the threads that tie our journeys together. Ultimately, this all comes together as part of the larger story we're creating, not just individually, but collectively.

Emanuel Gavert, Co-Founder of Vilde

The collision of seemingly random ideas is the catalyst for originality. The Collision Code is an enlightening guide to help you uncover the hidden opportunities for originality and offers a fresh perspective on forging meaningful connections that fuel creativity and collaboration.

Angus George, Executive Creative Director at Ogilvy UK

When we created Jazz Shapers, we wanted to celebrate founders who had intentionally broken the rules and defied convention to launch their businesses. Reading the Collision Code showed me how, without knowing it, we had given ourselves permission and the confidence to connect and attract our successful business shapers – people with the courage to back themselves and their ideas. This timely book is a must read for anyone looking to make it happen.

Elliot Moss, Partner and Chief Brand Officer at Mishcon de Reya

The Collision Code gives you simple and practical ways to help you be more connected. An easy and enjoyable read.

Dan Tatnall-Murray, Technical Specialist of Food and Agriculture of The United Nations

The Collision Code clearly explains the huge benefits from connecting with others and growing your network, through interesting examples and storytelling. As someone who helps others to make the most from networking, this is a great read for anyone looking for inspiration on how to make more meaningful connections.

Grace Fogarty, Presentation Skills Expert at Present with Grace Ltd

For me, *The Collision Code* is about giving yourself a chance, opening up to a world of endless and diverse possibilities. A chance encounter with James got me a job while I was a student, and taught me the power of making that initial connection.

Nick Johnston, Senior Manager at Macquarie Group

James' book, *The Collision Code*, is a powerful reminder to embrace life's opportunities and create meaningful connections before it's too late. His personal journey and insightful reflections inspire readers to take action now, live with intention, and build relationships that truly matter.

Fraser Doherty MBE, Founder of SuperJam and Co-Founder of Beer52

The Collision Code highlights the importance of self-leadership and how one person can create a ripple effect of impact. James' journey, as an AIESEC UK alumnus, is a testament to what can be achieved. With its relatable and inspiring stories, this book is essential reading for students aiming to stand out and take charge of their future.

Anka Grujic, Head of Business Development at AIESEC UK, 2024–25

Real-world connection is more important than ever, and in *The Collision Code* I can see that James has brought together all the elements that proved so successful when we worked together on the Kentish Cluster meet-ups. It's great to see these ideas for giving a community the permission, confidence and context to connect being shared more widely, and helping more people participate in or create communities of their own.

Tom Kihl, Managing Director at The Loco

Meeting James all those years ago on the underground platform perfectly captures *The Collision Code* in action. We're often surrounded by opportunities otherwise missed and by reading the book and leaning into the "code" it seems serendipity can really be unlocked.

Darren Ziff, Entrepreneur and Founder of Walk Eat London

The Collision Code brilliantly showcases the power of self-leadership and the incredible impact one person can have. As an AIESEC UK alumnus, James sets a powerful example for our members of what's possible when you take initiative and embrace opportunities. Filled with relatable and inspiring stories, it's a must-read for any student eager to get ahead and make their mark.

Michelle Chong, President of AIESEC UK, 2024–25

In a time of increasing isolation, this is a timely and important book. James Eder uses his own experiences—both the successes and the failures—to illustrate just how easy it can be to connect with others to move things that matter to you both forward in ways that would not be possible on your own. A must-read for anyone trying to get something big off the ground.

Edward Lamont, Team Performance Expert, Co-Author of TEAM: Getting Things Done with Others

The Collision Code is a masterclass in the art of serendipity—how the right connections, at the right time, can change everything. In a world obsessed with strategy and planning, this book is a refreshing reminder that the most transformative opportunities often arise from unexpected encounters. A must-read for anyone looking to harness the power of meaningful relationships in business and life.

Duncan Cheatle, Founder/Chairman of Learn Amp and Helm (previously The Supper Club), Co-founder of StartUp Britain

This book is an invitation to rethink how we connect. Some people seem to have a natural gift for creating serendipitous, meaningful interactions, but James shows that these moments aren't just luck—they can be intentionally designed. Drawing from his own real-world experiences, he shares compelling insights and practical strategies to help anyone cultivate connections that spark ideas, create opportunities and enrich life in unexpected ways.

Poonam Sakarsudha, Social Justice Consultant at The Meliorist

Biography

James Eder is an entrepreneur, work–life coach, public speaker and published author. He has over twenty years of experience in various leadership roles.

He is the co-founder of Student Beans, a lifestyle platform for university students which includes the latest deals and discounts, providing student verification technology to brands across the globe from the USA to Australia and beyond. In early 2024 the parent company re-branded to Pion which helps retail and eCommerce marketers make their brand relevant with youth, Gen Z and other valuable consumer groups. By combining insights, advertising and verification, Pion helps brands understand, engage and grow loyalty with their target consumers. *The Collision Code* gives an insight behind how James, with his co-founder and brother alongside the team, built the business on the foundation that people do business with people.

In 2005 he graduated from the University of Birmingham having completed his dissertation on "The Impact of Coaching in Organisations". Since then he has been on a continuous self-development journey sharing his experience and knowledge as a mentor and coaching people helping support their own adventures. In 2021 James completed an ACC ICF accredited programme with Optimus Coach Academy. In March 2024 he published an Amazon number one best-selling book *The Power of Coaching* written alongside nine other graduates from Optimus Coach Academy.

James is a frequent speaker delivering interactive sessions at conferences, schools and universities across the UK and internationally on subjects including startups, entrepreneurship, resilience, serendipity and networking.

Following the discovery of his heart condition, hypertrophic cardiomyopathy, he has designed a life to work for him. Most recently James focuses his time leveraging his experience and expertise as a work–life coach delivering transformation for his clients. Focusing on entrepreneurs and founders and people who know they want to make a change in their lives, he gives them SAS: space, accountability and support to help them be the best they already are.

Biography

Don't Be a Stranger

I really hope you enjoyed reading *The Collision Code* and joining me on this journey.

If I can help with anything or you'd like to share any thoughts or feedback with me feel free to connect with me:

LinkedIn: https://www.linkedin.com/in/jameseder/

Email: james@thecollisioncode.com

Web: www.thecollisioncode.com

Instagram: https://www.instagram.com/thecollisioncode/

If you have a story you want to share online about the collisions you've made, feel free to tag us on Instagram @thecollisioncode #thecollisioncode #sayhello.

Printed in Dunstable, United Kingdom